ROME

By E. R. Chamberlin
and the Editors of Time-Life Books

Photographs by Dan Budnik

THE GREAT CITIES · TIME-LIFE BOOKS · AMSTERDAM

The Author: E. R. Chamberlin, born in Kingston, Jamaica, in 1926, now lives in England. Of his 14 previously published books, two are specifically concerned with Rome, *The Bad Popes* and *The Fall of the House of Borgia.* His first contact with Rome was made during the Holy Year of 1950 when he journeyed on foot to the city from his home in England. The trip took six months and gave him an intimate view of Europe and, particularly, Italy. Over the following years he returned again and again to Rome, building up a personal view of the city.

The Photographer: Dan Budnik was born on Long Island, New York, in 1933. He studied painting at New York City's Art Students' League, where he developed his interest in photography. After spending two years in the army, he began a career in photojournalism. Budnik has taken photographs for most of the leading international magazines and has contributed extensively to TIME-LIFE Books.

EDITOR: Dale Brown
Picture Editor: Pamela Marke
Assistant Picture Editor: Anne Angus
Design Consultant: Louis Klein
Staff Writer: Deborah Thompson
Researchers: Gunn Brinson, Vanessa Kramer, Jackie Matthews, Jasmine Spencer
Designer: Graham Davis
Assistant Designer: Roy Williams
Design Assistant: Shirin Patel
Picture Assistants: Cathy Doxat-Pratt, Christine Hinze

The captions and text of the picture essays were written by the staff of TIME-LIFE Books

Valuable assistance was given in the preparation of this volume by TIME-LIFE Correspondent Ann Natanson, Rome.

Published by TIME-LIFE International (Nederland) B.V.
5 Ottho Heldringstraat, Amsterdam 18

Cover: Early-morning shadows streak the pale cascade of the Spanish Steps, a symbol of Rome for generations of visitors.

First end paper: As part of their ordination, young priests prostrate themselves in St. Peter's Square to show their humility.

Last end paper: In the Camposanto al Verano, the largest cemetery in Rome, niches contain simple memorials to the dead.

TIME LIFE BOOKS

THE WORLD'S WILD PLACES
HUMAN BEHAVIOUR
THE ART OF SEWING
THE OLD WEST
THE EMERGENCE OF MAN
LIFE LIBRARY OF PHOTOGRAPHY
TIME-LIFE LIBRARY OF ART
FOODS OF THE WORLD
GREAT AGES OF MAN
LIFE SCIENCE LIBRARY
LIFE NATURE LIBRARY

Contents

I

The Eternal Riddle

The railway from Florence to Rome runs through some of the most beautiful country in the world; but it's a long journey, and after three hours you have had enough. Then you can feel a stir of interest as the train meets the Tiber—a sinuous flood that flows companionably alongside. People start collecting their belongings. Some cross to the right-hand side of the train for a first glimpse of Rome. What they see is merely the high embankment of the new ring road. But fortunately it looks for all the world like a city wall; and beyond it the cypresses of the Campo Verano cemetery seem suitably classical. It's on the other side of the train that the first monument appears—the graceful Porta Maggiore, islanded now among tramlines but unchanged since the early romantic travellers saw it, with grass and flowers growing out of its stone. And now the city is all around you: there's a glimpse of a street market, a golden statue on a towering column, an anonymous ruin—and at last the high, echoing vaults of the station.

This, surely, is the best way to enter Rome. You can come in by air of course. But of all modern transport, the railway is surely the one that the builders of ancient Rome would have adopted as their own. Thunderous yet precise, swooping down from the North to slip through a gap in the walls, the train comes to a halt in the heart of the city. And the modern station itself has all the contrasts that characterize Rome. Beneath the splendid, casual undulation of the roof is an almost futuristic world of glass and metal where you can eat, drink and even have a bath. But if you descend to the *Metropolitana* below, you will immediately strike the very roots of the city, for the stairs pass the base of an immense brown wall. Servius Tullius, one of Rome's early kings, is credited with building this wall in the 6th Century B.C., circling the city with its solid protection at a time when the town was still besieged by enemies. But the enemies were pushed far back beyond the limits of the homeland and the wall fell into disuse. Battered and gradually hidden over the centuries, it was brought to light in our own day. But curiously, this fragment below the station is now reverently protected by glass, and the same wall rears into the open air above the station, exposed to wind and rain and the scratchers of graffiti.

The orderliness of the station ends at the great glass doors. Beyond its forecourt spreads a huge open space, not a piazza but simply an absence of buildings, filled with the murderous Roman traffic and the insouciant Roman pedestrians. To reach the city centre you must cross the lethal area. And here, at the very gate of Rome, you can see the difference between the Roman and the non-Roman.

Those young people, chattering like starlings as they drift across the road, seemingly unaware of the onrushing traffic, can only be Roman. But the man or woman who waits paralysed for a break in the traffic, or cringes as some monster bears down at twice the legal speed, is as likely to come from Milan as from London, from Bologna as from New York.

The approach by rail is best, but it was not always so. About a century ago, shortly after the railway was built, a visitor to Rome contrasted the new with the old approach to the city. "Those who arrive at Rome now by the railway . . . cannot imagine the effect which the words '*Ecco Roma*' (Behold Rome) formerly produced when, on arriving at the point in the road from which the Eternal City could be described for the first time. The postilion stopped his horses, and, pointing it out to the traveller in the distance, pronounced them with that Roman accent which is as grave and sonorous as the name of Rome itself." The great consular roads that run from Rome across the once lovely *Campagna*, the roads whose names sound a drum-roll of Roman history—Flaminia, Salaria, Nomentana, Appia, Cassia are built up now and choked with traffic. But from each there is still a point at which Rome breaks suddenly on the vision.

It was from the north—the Via Cassia—that I had my first view of Rome, on a September morning in 1950. I had hitch-hiked to the city from Orvieto. Clinging to the back of a rickety lorry as it climbed up and down the empty countryside, and not expecting anything in particular as we crested yet another hill, I suddenly became aware of an enormous, hemispherical object on the skyline. In any other city it would have been a gas or water tank. But this was Rome and the large, round object was the dome of St. Peter's, huge, golden and apparently insubstantial for it seemed to float in the warm autumn sky. It filled the horizon as we dipped down through the scented air into the next trough and then it was gone, and the lorry was chugging its way through suburban streets.

This vision of St. Peter's had to sustain me not only during that visit but for many years afterwards, because I did not fall in love with Rome at first sight. Presumably I proceeded on down the Via Flaminia, through the great Porta del Popolo, past the obelisk with its melancholy little lions spouting water and so on through the streets radiating beyond. I say presumably for I remember nothing of the first day after that almost symbolic glimpse of the dome. And my initial impression of the city was of an incoherent 19th-Century metropolis stuck round with shreds of marble and deformed by the ruins of huge brick buildings like blitzed warehouses.

Those brick ruins, in fact, are the ideal symbol for the city: time and again the marble and gilt have been torn off but the bricks underneath—the ugly, enduring bricks, the foundations of Rome—remain. I was in no mood to appreciate this at the time. I had come to Rome, with too high hopes—or perhaps I had travelled too slowly down the peninsula. The journey had taken me about four or five months, and I had come to know the cities

The indomitable character of Romans past and present is powerfully depicted in the stalwart demeanour of three matrons leaning against a barricade in St. Peter's Square. Their black dress reflects the ancient custom of remaining in permanent mourning after a loved one dies.

strung out like jewels along the roads. Verona, Mantua, Bologna, Florence, Siena, Orvieto—each was an organic whole, each was comprehensible although its parts were richly varied.

It wasn't that Rome overwhelmed me with its size. The Rome that the visitor knows, the Rome that we really mean by "Rome", is a small town: the population within the walls today is scarcely 150,000 and it is perfectly possible to walk across the heart, from the southern to the northern walls, within a morning. No, it wasn't size—Naples is almost as big; Milan even bigger. Nor was I impressed by the city's age: because that almost oppressive sense of history comes only gradually, after days of exploration. And many of the other Italian cities seem, at first glance, much older than Rome.

One reason why Rome yields itself grudgingly, if at all, to the hurried or casual visitor may be the apparent lack of continuity, the juxtaposition in space of buildings separated by centuries in time. Twice almost within memory the face of the city has been drastically changed. The first occasion was in 1870 when Rome became the capital of a united Italy. The population rocketed, immigrants poured in, and spaces that had been green since the beginning of Rome were suddenly occupied by masses of mediocre buildings. Again in the 1930s an ambitious town-planning programme severed past from present in many vulnerable parts of the city. It is impossible not to regret the loss of intimate streets that were swept away to create the Via della Conciliazione that now connects St. Peter's with the river in a dead straight line. The hurried visitor is only too likely to carry away in his mind a pattern, of triumphal avenues and boulevards, without any sense of the city's age or of its present vivid life.

A large part of the literature in Rome reflects this fact. Many who later loved the city have left bewildered, or even contemptuous, accounts of their first hours of contact. "It is not the contrast of pig-sties and palaces that I complain of", wrote the English essayist William Hazlitt. "What I object to is the want of any such striking contrast but an almost uninterrupted succession of narrow, vulgar looking streets where the smell of garlic prevails over the odour of antiquity." Charles Dickens rather glumly thought that Rome looked just like the dingy London of his day. And the artist Whistler exploded: "Ruins don't count. This is only a stucco-town. I am going." And off he went.

Still, there is an ambiguity, a kind of love-hate, in most visitors' first impressions of Rome. The American author Nathaniel Hawthorne summed up this reaction when he described how he, too, first hated and then inexplicably found himself loving the city. "When we have once known Rome and left her where she lies, like a decaying corpse—left her in utter weariness, no doubt, of her narrow, crooked, intricate streets, into which the sun never falls . . . we are astonished by the discovery, by and by, that our heartstrings have mysteriously attached themselves to the Eternal City and are drawing us thitherward again."

Two pedestrians test their nerve on the traffic-filled Largo Argentina, where true Romans distinguish themselves by their cool bravado against a sea of cars.

A major obstacle to understanding Rome is the special character of the city's inhabitants, who are inclined to keep to themselves and thus to keep the city to themselves. On a later visit to Rome I found myself at dinner one evening, seated next to an elderly American. He had been born Italian, could switch in mid-thought from one language to another, and moved among foreign idioms as gracefully as he moved among his own. During our conversation we circled, as it were, around the Roman character by considering the citizens of other city-states. The Milanese? "They're businessmen. They work hard, play hard. They'll pay for entertainment but expect good value for money." Venetians? They, he said, were witty, canny, drank heavily. Florentines? He was contemptuous of these darlings of Western civilization. "They're merchants, traders. They'd take the shirt off your back with a smile. They hate spending money. Their idea of entertainment is to go for a long walk." Piedmontese? "*Falsita e cortesia*—I wouldn't trust 'em an inch. The same goes for the Neapolitans—only they'll at least cheat you with a laugh. The Neapolitan will go to immense trouble to beat you out of a few lire, but won't be resentful if you get the better of him. Not that you're likely to. Sienese? Haughty. Very high opinion of themselves, but generous enough. Pisans? Quarrelsome."

And the Romans? "Ah, the Romans. They're difficult to get to know. They never really accept the foreigner—and a Milanese is as much a foreigner as an Englishman. You'll never enter their homes. No Italian really likes to bring people into his house, but the Roman won't even consider it. There's his private life and his public life. And his public life includes quite close friends—the kind of friend that an Englishman or American would include in his home circle. And as for outsiders—we only belong to a parallel world. You can't blame them, really: they've seen too many of us come and go."

He made a good point there. No metropolis is friendly to the stranger; it is too much to expect its citizens to react humanely to yet another meaningless face in the street. And Rome has seen too many new faces, too often and for too long. Since the days of the Caesars the city has been the goal of gawky provincials. Even in the Dark Ages so many pilgrims came to Rome that guide books were produced for their benefit. Year after year, century after century, the pilgrims flooded down the peninsula. The invasion started just before Easter and did not end until just after Christmas. Even today, only during the three dead months of winter can the Romans call the city their own. At times the foreigners actually outnumber the natives, and in sheer self-defence the Romans have evolved their own specialized method of coping with the intrusion.

The Roman defence is based upon the ancient virtue called *gravitas*, whose outward sign is taciturnity. The foreigner is deemed to be invisible, inaudible and, apart from the unfortunate accident of actually occupying space, insubstantial. A Roman, asked for the tenth time that day to point

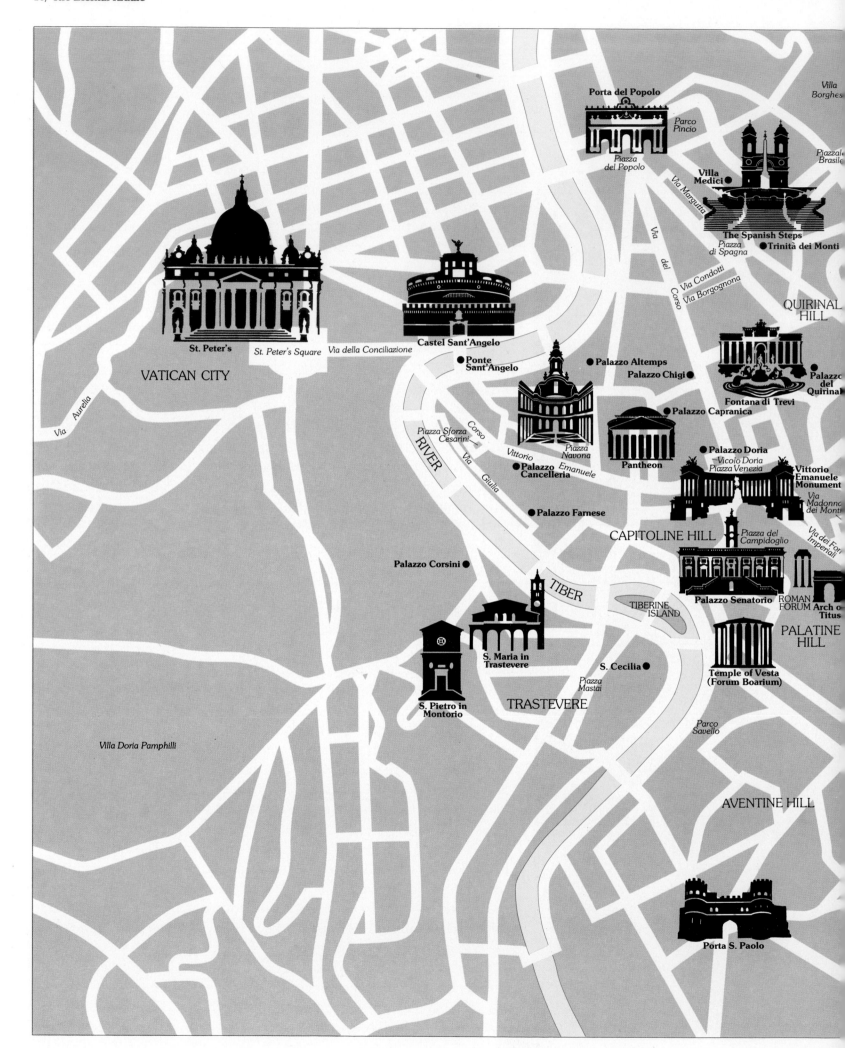

Villa Borghes

Porta del Popolo

Parco Pincio

Piazza del Popolo

Piazzal Brasile

Villa Medici ●

The Spanish Steps

Piazza di Spagna

● **Trinità dei Monti**

Via Margutta

St. Peter's

St. Peter's Square

Castel Sant'Angelo

Via della Conciliazione

● **Ponte Sant'Angelo**

● **Palazzo Altemps**

Palazzo Chigi ●

VATICAN CITY

Via del Corso

Via Condotti

Via Borgognona

QUIRINAL HILL

Via Aurelia

Piazza Sforza Cesarini

Corso

Via Giulia

RIVER

Vittorio

● **Palazzo Cancelleria**

Piazza Navona

Emanuele

Pantheon

● **Palazzo Capranica**

Fontana di Trevi

● **Palazzo del Quirinal**

● **Palazzo Doria**

Vicolo Doria

Piazza Venezia

Vittorio Emanuele Monument

Via Madonna dei Monti

● **Palazzo Farnese**

Piazza del Campidoglio

CAPITOLINE HILL

Via dei Fori Imperiali

Palazzo Corsini ●

TIBER

TIBERINE ISLAND

Palazzo Senatorio

ROMAN FORUM

Arch of Titus

S. Maria in Trastevere

S. Cecilia ●

Temple of Vesta (Forum Boarium)

PALATINE HILL

S. Pietro in Montorio

Piazza Mastai

TRASTEVERE

Parco Savello

Villa Doria Pamphilli

AVENTINE HILL

Porta S. Paolo

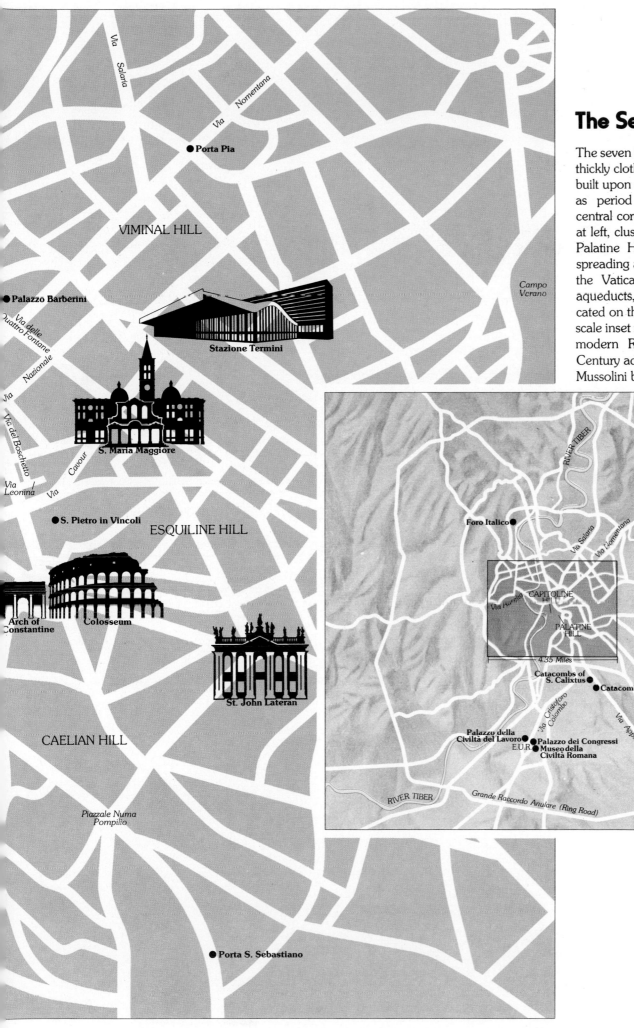

The Seven Historic Hills

The seven hills of Rome beside the Tiber are thickly clothed with the edifices of centuries, built upon or incorporated into one another as period succeeded period. The city's central core is shown in the schematic map at left, clustered around the Capitoline and Palatine Hills as it was in antiquity, and spreading across the river to St. Peter's and the Vatican. Important features—piazzas, aqueducts, temples, churches—are indicated on the larger map, while on the small-scale inset map below is shown the extent of modern Rome, complete with its 20th-Century additions, such as E.U.R., the "city" Mussolini built in the southern suburbs.

out the way for a foreigner whose language might be Chinese, English or Turkish, has long since learnt to do so with a minimum of energy. He indicates silently—why cast linguistic pearls before swine? A gesture of a hand and a movement of the head will suffice. In shops or offices, he volunteers no information whatsoever for this would merely produce more demands: so the questioner himself must frame the necessary demands. Do you close at lunchtime? Yes. Do you re-open in the afternoon? Yes. At what time? 3.30. . . . Indeed, if the information is printed on a notice tacked to a wall the questioner will receive no reply at all, simply an index finger pointing rigidly to the notice.

But the blank look and the taciturnity are self-protective, not hostile or indifferent. Should circumstances demand, there can be a sudden warm reaction. My wife once felt ill as we were nearing the end of a meal in a restaurant. In a moment the entire staff had rushed to her aid, carried her into a back room, proffered cordials and smelling salts, summoned a taxi. Only when we were speeding away did I realize that no one had mentioned the large bill we had incurred. When I returned to pay it next day, I learned that it had not been forgotten: to have presented it the previous night would not have been civilized. The street singers who haunt the restaurants, the cripples at the street corners, the gipsy girls with their beautiful, grubby children maintain their lives largely at the expense of spontaneous Roman generosity. But the need has to be real: the foreigner who has merely lost his way or his wallet must make what he can out of a shrugged shoulder, an inclined head, a pointing finger.

In time, this taciturnity can be seen, in fact, as a kind of courtesy. On entering Rome after a prolonged stay in Tuscany you miss the easy conversation of strangers, the amiable "*buon appetito*" as you sit down to a meal, the courteous greeting with which the shopkeeper hails your entry. But, in compensation, you are free from any irritating curiosity. "*Dica.*" The Roman shopkeeper booms as you step over his threshold: "Speak"—no nonsense about good day, or good evening, but simply the phrase for "State your requirements". The Roman pays the foreigner the compliment of assuming that he has his own affairs to attend to, that he can perfectly well look after himself. As a result, no matter how bizarre he may appear to be, the stranger melts into the background and can get on with his own business in any part of the city.

Such was the picture I built up of the Roman and his city over ten years or so but it was like dissecting a watch. I still lacked the warmth towards the city that could come only from personal involvement. But when it came at last, it was a profound change: and it was triggered by a trivial circumstance.

On this occasion I arrived in Rome in mid-August, that most hideous of Roman months. It was all that I had feared: the streets crowded, the air heavy with exhaust fumes, the city gasping. Unwisely, I did as the Romans do, and ate a prolonged midday meal with lots of wine. (Rome is blessed in the deceptively mild, full-bodied white wines of the Castelli, from the nearby Alban hills.) At mid-afternoon I emerged from the cool restaurant into a heat that felt like a physical weight on my back and shoulders. I dodged from patch of shade to patch of shade as if from shelter to shelter in a violent rainstorm. At last I found myself on the Capitoline Hill above the Roman Forum, and saw that behind Michelangelo's formal square there was a little park. Tall pines brought a scent of the country, and banks of purple and crimson oleanders overhung a few seats. Deciding to leave the city at the earliest opportunity, I sank down in one of the seats and fell asleep.

An hour later I was wakened by the most pleasant breeze I have ever felt. Afterwards I was to know it as the *ponentino*, the westerly. In prosaic terms it is simply a wind rising from the sea 15 miles distant. Some trick of the hills and river sends it scouring through Rome at the worst hours of the day. Even if you are trapped in a cul-de-sac or a car-choked alley it reaches out, touches and revives you. I got up, thirsty, and heard the second miracle— the sound of water falling; water even at this height above the city. Tracing the sound, I found one of the small bronze wolves of Rome whose jaws spout refreshment day and night. Defying *every* canon of southern travel, I drank and found the water cold and sweet, not simply a way of ending thirst, but a sensual experience, a taste as positive as any wine. The flow went on and on. I washed and drank and splashed, then turned back to the little park. It was, in fact, a garden on the summit of the Tarpeian rock, an ancient place of execution, but innocent to the eye as is so much that has sinister associations in Rome. Beyond the valley of the Forum the cypresses on the Palatine Hill rose like enormous green candle flames. The glare had gone from the sky: it showed hints of the daily splendour called the Roman sunset. There seemed no reason why these factors should combine into a significant whole. But they did: and Rome was, for me, born in that instant.

A High Perspective

The Spanish Steps ripple elegantly down from the church of the Trinità dei Monti (left) to the Piazza di Spagna, where two umbrellas shade the flower stalls.

It is a city built to be looked at: its splendid vistas have been designed expressly as a setting fit for daily pomp and ceremony. These aerial photographs, almost all taken on a single early morning helicopter flight over the centre of Rome, show some of the city's most familiar landmarks, and they record the greatest periods of its history—the ancient empire, the 16th- and 17th-Century flowering of papal power and the 19th-

Century emergence of Italian nationalism. Now, at this early hour, the piazzas are almost empty, and the usually thronged Spanish Steps (above) are deserted. Even the swirling traffic, already beginning its daily turmoil, dwindles into insignificance when seen remotely from above. In the pellucid summer air that is one of Rome's most magical qualities, fountains, churches and obelisks rise clear and unencumbered.

Across the Piazza del Popolo twin domed churches (left), completed in the 1670s, face the ceremonial gate (far right) where the Via Flaminia enters Rome.

The Spaces of Welcome

Piazzas like theatrical sets were the delight of powerful popes, and of the architects they commissioned to adorn their city. Laid out to impress the pilgrims, envoys and foreign rulers visiting the city, the Piazza del Popolo (above) was the first sight to greet the eyes of a traveller arriving by road from the north; and the Piazza San Pietro (right) met the visitor approaching St. Peter's itself. From above, they appear as clear as a designer's blueprint.

The vast colonnaded circle that spreads before St. Peter's was designed and built by Bernini, foremost of Baroque architects, for Pope Alexander VII (1655-67).

The Piazza Navona, once an ancient racecourse, was remodelled in the 17th Century by Pope Innocent X.

Reincarnations of the Imperial Past

Once-glorious landmarks of ancient Rome, battered into oblivion during the Dark Ages and medieval times, reappeared after the Renaissance, transformed under the hands of men imbued with a new sense of the greatness of their own age. Above, the original curving lines of an ancient stadium survive in a Baroque piazza; right, Michelangelo's harmonious design of palaces and pavement dignifies the Capitol, the hill that was the centre of ancient Rome.

An aerial view reveals all the delicacy of Michelangelo's elliptical star-patterned pavement in the Piazza del Campidoglio, designed in 1536 for Pope Paul III.

King Vittorio Emanuele's monument, begun in 1885 and completed in 1911, flanks the Capitol to the north.

Monuments of Kingdom and Empire

Towering above its surroundings, the massive Vittorio Emanuele monument (above), erected in the very heart of Rome's most ancient quarter, commemorates the political unification of Italy into a kingdom in 1870. Its self-sufficient entity contrasts almost grotesquely with the strewn stones of the ruined Roman Forum (right), which lies only yards away over the Capitoline Hill, like the untidy plundered graveyard of a past civilization.

At either end of the Forum two huge arches survive: that of Titus (foreground), built in A.D. 81, and that of Septimius Severus (background), dated A.D. 203.

Minuscule cars circulate round the ruins of the Colosseum, majestic even in decay. The huge amphitheatre, opened in A.D. 80, held 45,000 spectators.

2

The Roman in his Habitat

My first visits to Rome tended to be brief, each consisting of a few days at most, conducted almost in the spirit of a raid in quest of some specific objective. But as I began to succumb to the city's lure, I wanted to go behind the surface, to sense Rome's regular pulse beneath the confusion and ambiguity. The only way to do that was to bury myself for a time in some district that was central but relatively free of tourists. The ancient, undeniably down at heel but quintessentially Roman Suburra, just a few hundred yards north of the Colosseum, seemed to be the ideal for the purpose. Here I lived for several weeks, feeling out the rhythms of daily life amid the working-class shabbiness of the Suburra's dun-coloured buildings, narrow black-paved lanes and clusters of small shops, and most of all in the natural habitat of the Roman: the restaurant.

The Suburra is something of an anomaly. It is perhaps the most ancient inhabited area of the city, but few maps bother to identify it, and only the more dedicated guidebooks even refer to it. It has been cut adrift from the rest of the city. Once the long, narrow street that today goes under the names of the Via Leonina (at the eastern end) and Via Madonna dei Monti (near the western end) ran straight as a die to the great Forum, the square that was the hub of Ancient Rome. But in the 1st Century A.D. the emperor Nerva severed the link by dumping his own forum squarely across the road's course. The separation was made permanent when Mussolini carved his massive Via dei Fori Imperiali along the side of the ancient Forum; now the Suburra's western boundary is sealed by lethal streams of traffic. Although the eastern boundary has become indeterminate, the other two are almost as clear-cut and modern as Mussolini's monument to Fascism: to the south, the Via Cavour, pompous, fussy, depressing; to the north, the Via Nazionale, cheerful and well-mannered, its bustling shops giving it something of a Parisian air.

The Suburra proper gives the impression of density, of homogeneity; buildings crowding the streets without any fringe of trees or flowers to provide colour. It is a secretive, inward looking, working-man's area. It is also, not surprisingly, a staunch Communist stronghold, but of the typically Italian kind; flexible, sophisticated, owing as much to Machiavelli as to Marx, but with a veneer all its own.

I recall falling into conversation with a burly young demolition worker who, a few moments earlier, had been balanced on a rickety-looking wall, attacking the bricks with a pick. Something glittered on his chest—swinging as he swung—a necklace with a cross. It must have been a nuisance, but he

Following the Roman tradition of turning ancient buildings to new uses, instead of tearing them down, a butcher's shop occupies an alcove in an antique wall. The marble door frame may have come from the remains of the near-by Portico of Octavia, which Augustus dedicated to his sister Octavia in 23 B.C.

said that he never removed it. Yet he was a Communist, an active Party member. "But how can you wear that round your neck?" He answered with finality, "Christ I love: but the priests and rich men I don't like." His sentiments had the authentic ring of the true Roman, for whom anticlericalism—in a city where the Pope is a living presence—is often the reverse side of a passionate faith.

My *pensione* was in the Via degli Zingari, deep in the heart of the anonymous blocks of flats whose shape hasn't changed since the days of the Caesars. This one could have been 50 or 500 years old. It was impossible to tell, for its appearance outside was that of an austere rectangle, punctuated with three rows of windows, and no part of it had seen a paint brush for decades. The interior walls had a patchy, leprous look but the woodwork had faded to a pleasant silver-blond. This was the locus from which I chose to experience the Suburra.

Six o'clock in the morning: sleep is shattered by a rasping crash that prolongs itself in the street outside. By hanging out of the window at a dangerous angle, I find it just possible to see the cause of the noise: an immense load of firewood being delivered to the shop next door. It seems remarkable that in this semi-industrial working class area there should be any need for so vast a quantity of logs. But many residents of the Suburra still rely on this form of fuel. And in the evening, when the cooking for supper begins, the air becomes as fragrant with woodsmoke as that of a mountain village. All self-respecting cooks still use wood; even the chefs in the marble and chromium tourist traps near the Roman Forum fire their pizza ovens with wood.

Thus rudely awakened, I head for the bathroom. The handle comes off the bedroom door. It always comes off if you forget to press down as you pull. In the corridor a pink bedside light burns day and night, winter and summer. From the bathroom you can peer down into a deep courtyard, round which the pension is built. It is a dingy wall with tiny windows rimming it. At one of the windows someone has hung out a bunch of red peppers; the glowing red of the fruit and the deep green of the leaves give a splash of heraldic colour. Downstairs there is another unexpected touch. At the street door a threadbare red carpet has been laid on the lower flight of stone steps. At intervals along the carpet are placed enormous pots of white lilies. The flowers and the carpet seem to light up the whole entrance, and for the first time I notice that the lines of the building are elegant.

The street door, usually double locked, has been thrown back; so too has the metal grille behind it. The whole world, if it wishes, can walk in and out. For all this display is in honour of a wedding, and the thieves who infest the area would never take advantage of that wide-open door: it is bad luck to steal from the house of a bride (that's the theory, anyway). The bride is a sallow girl, with a silent mother and a garrulous father. The family lives on

The Virgin's gilded aura brightens a dark passageway, the Via S. Francesco di Paola, in the old, crowded Suburra district where dense shadow can hold even Rome's intense midday sun at bay. The steps run from the Via Cavour, a modern street, to the Church of S. Pietro in Vincoli, which contains chains said to have bound St. Peter before his crucifixion.

the top floor. The father is something in the tax office, which puts him a cut above the small traders and craftsmen of the locality, although his income is probably less than half theirs, and this display for his daughter's wedding is intended to reflect his status.

It is not yet seven o'clock, but the street life of the Via degli Zingari is already in full swing. A dynamo whines in the small garage, and the cabinet-maker's mallet taps next door. The *trattoria* on the corner won't be open for several hours yet, but the bar of the general store, which doubles as a café, is crowded with Romans gulping their breakfast. The Roman café is not a place for dawdling. Those cafés that copy the languorous northern custom of putting out tables and chairs on the pavement are patronized for the most part by foreigners. The Romans use a café as a fuelling station on their way to work, a place to prepare for the day with a thimbleful of thick, sweet coffee and a sticky cake, finished in a moment.

The proprietor of this café-cum-grocer's shop serves coffee, spirits, wine and the occasional beer every day except Monday, when he closes "for the weekly repose", as his printed notice informs his customers. His shop is like the village shop of everybody's childhood. You can buy soap in great yellow wedges, or cheese that looks like the soap; you can buy tiny green peas and inflatable rubber ducks, raw-looking ham and postcards showing dark-haired beauties languishing in moonlight. Near the till are three enormous, incredibly expensive teddy-bears. Presumably some drunk will eventually buy one as a peace offering to an enraged wife. But he won't be a local. There is also a row of bottles of very expensive foreign liquors. They look as though they have been there since the shop was built: and they will probably remain there until the Colosseum falls. Every Roman café has this Bacchic shrine: evidently it serves to demonstrate the proprietor's status, his ability to lock up capital indefinitely; for the bottles are never broached and very rarely bought.

The proprietor—a burly, sardonic man—speaks a dialect that is almost incomprehensible to me. These encounters with an unknown species of Italian are among those Roman experiences that are, for the foreigner, supremely disconcerting. No doubt he has honourably set about learning text-book Italian, and in the process he has digested the information that the ideal form of the language for Rome is a "*lingua Toscana in bocca romana*"—a Tuscan vocabulary pronounced in the Roman manner. He has then discovered that every third Roman is speaking something that might as well be Chinese. The reason is simple. The city is flooded with immigrants from the rest of the peninsula, mainly from the South. They have been pouring in since the turn of the century; they far outnumber the original Romans; and they cling to the dialects of their birthplace.

My proprietor is *Calabrese*. One could perhaps guess that from the dusty, higgledy-piggledy condition of his shop. But the bar gleams. In this, at least, he has done as the Romans do. The stainless steel of the serving

Relaxing in the warm night, a crowd of people enjoy a particular Roman pleasure: a late and leisurely dinner out of doors in a piazza in the Trastevere district. Behind the tables the 18th-Century façade of the church of Quaranta Martiri rises into the soft darkness.

area is wiped down every few minutes; the glittering implements seem more like ornaments than tools. And when he takes over the coffee machine from his wife, it is with the air of a pilot settling himself at the controls of a Jumbo jet.

At eight o'clock the little Via Leonina that runs parallel with the Via degli Zingari is flooded with clerkly figures, disgorged by the *Metro* at the bottom of the street and now taking a short cut to the shops and offices on the Via Nazionale. The flood recedes, and by nine o'clock the Suburra is left to its own devices—to earn a living in its own fashion as it has done for the past 2,000 years or so.

In the short length of the Via Leonina and its sister street Via degli Zingari there are nearly 40 businesses, many of them side by side: a tiny printer's; a cobbler's; an antique shop; two or three garages or cycle repair shops; a leather worker; a weaver of basketry; a maker of handbags and umbrellas; innumerable food shops—bakers, wine and oil, pizza. But, ominously, there are almost as many shops closed as open, for the Suburra is suffering the fate that is afflicting all central Rome—a drastic decline in population. Perhaps 40 per cent of the people who used to live and work here ten years ago have moved out to the suburbs. The unfashionable Suburra has not yet undergone the transformation that more desirable areas are experiencing: the conversion of the workman's home into a trendy executive's house, the intrusion of offices and prestige showrooms. And there is something missing, an absence painfully noticeable in any Italian town: the sight and sound of children at play. Increasingly this is becoming an area of the elderly, of those who cling to the locality where they were born but who will not be replaced when they pass on.

The few children who remain may be seen in what is the real heart of the Suburra: the small, informal Piazza Madonna dei Monti: and that is because of its fountain. An attraction as well as a playground, the fountain looks completely out of place in the scruffy piazza. It is the centre for a small street market; an orange box or a couple of plastic bags usually float in the green water, and the fountain's steps are garnished with unwanted vegetables. Altogether, the fountain looks like a dowager duchess who has strayed into rough company and doesn't quite know how to detach herself —one of Rome's endless contradictions. Giacomo della Porta, the sculptor and architect, made the fountain in 1588, and for centuries it was fed by an aqueduct with the happy name of Acqua Felice—the sole water supply for the tangle of small streets round about. In summer it is the delight of the area's small boys. Brown and lithe as eels, they splash in its generous basin while their prettily dressed sisters look on wistfully. By Roman *mores*, boys will be boys, but little girls must be little ladies.

At midday the rhythm of life in the Suburra begins to slow down as the city enters the trance—the coma of the three midday hours known (with a touch of irony) as the lunch "hour". In this institution, certainly, Rome proclaims that it is a southern city more akin to Athens or Algiers than to Florence or Milan. All Italian cities tend to nod off around the hour of the midday meal, with the shops closed, the traffic stilled. But Rome plunges into an uninhibited slumber, cutting the day into two at the meridian. The hiatus is an institution that tests the tolerance of the foreigner to the utmost: government offices will not open again that day, nor will most galleries and museums. One of the sadder sights of the city is the scarlet-faced tourist who, intent on "doing" Rome in a day or so, has lunched too early and too quickly and now finds himself tramping the streets of a dead city in which every door is closed to him.

Every door, that is, except the door of the *trattoria*, the *osteria* and the *ristorante*. Unlike the hotel or *pensione*, which caters solely for the stranger, the Roman restaurant exists basically for the Roman. Here he leads his public life. This is the place to relax, and, in the mellow company of a little wine, observe both patrons and clients alike. As someone once remarked to me, "If you want to see the Roman at home, as it were, then go to any restaurant. That's the true Roman entertainment." So I did—often.

Along the unfashionable streets within a few hundred yards from Piazza Madonna dei Monti, there are some 15 eating houses. At the far end, where the Via del Boschetto joins the bustling Via Nazionale, these establishments boast two or three waiters in white jackets, mountains of fruit in baskets, printed menus and painted scenes upon the walls. But as you travel away from the Via Nazionale towards the core of the Suburra, you descend in the social scale until you come to "Angelo's". This is the archetypal eating house, with the *Signora* in the kitchen and the *Padrone* in the dining-room and paper tablecloths on the tables. Custom in "Angelo's" is always bad, but not much worse than in any other *trattoria* in the area. During the lunch hour there will probably be a couple of building workers washing the brick dust out of their throats with half a litre of Angelo's thin, cloudy wine, a clerk having a cheap meal as a treat, and, very occasionally, a tourist. The *trattoria* is well positioned, for it is tucked in an attractive corner of the Piazza Madonna dei Monti where tourists often stray. But Angelo makes no attempt to exploit either the position or the foreigners. They are charged, and treated, exactly the same as the locals. There is no written menu, for it is assumed that you know what's available. If requested, Angelo will reel off the names of the dishes that his wife has prepared; but since he speaks dialect in a slurred monotone with his own abbreviations, the average tourist is left no wiser.

Husband and wife form the basic unit of the street-corner *trattoria* in the Suburra. The pattern is maintained even in the more fashionable eating-places towards the Via Nazionale, although there the wife may have left the oven for the cash-desk. In the busier evening hours a grown-up son or nephew—never a daughter or niece—will lend a hand as waiter, and after the evening rush he will entertain his friends as payment in kind. When no

Rome is a city where freshness of food matters. Here a Trastevere restaurant-owner returns from the fish market with his carefully selected purchases under white napkins. Fish is a popular fare in Rome, and local restaurateurs who know their regular customers' tastes cater directly to their preferences.

relative is available, a waiter is reluctantly hired but he is hedged about with minute regulations. I gave up using one otherwise excellent *trattoria*, embarrassed by the humiliation of the solitary waiter, a well-set-up, melancholy man in his late fifties. He was allowed no responsibility whatsoever: if his customer wanted even a piece of cheese, solemnly the waiter would have to trundle the cheese to the *Signora* in the kitchen, where she would carve off the necessary amount and send him back with it. He could change no bank-note above a certain denomination without the permission of the *Padrone*, who would ritually inspect the note, scrutinize the customer and then dismiss the waiter with a nod. In between serving, the wretched man would stand like a clockwork toy that had run down, ignored by everyone.

The *pranzo*, the midday meal, is a practical, hasty affair. Not so the *cena*, the last meal of the day. The evening meal begins late—as late as 9 or even 10 p.m.—and goes on to midnight or later. It is not so much that the diner is eating vast quantities of food—although the courses are certainly generous enough—as the fact that the service is incredibly leisurely. This is not immediately obvious: on the contrary, when the diner enters he is pounced upon and swept to a table; the wine glasses are turned up with a flourish, orders are taken, bread, wine and water are brought, all as though it were intended to break a speed record. And then nothing. This is the period during which the Roman adjusts to a relaxed tempo if he is dining alone. In every restaurant there are the solitary diners, each islanded at an individual table, pensively nibbling bread to keep the pangs of hunger at bay, contemplating the day's affairs perhaps, or just blankly awaiting the first course. It is easy to spot the foreigner—and this includes the Milanese and Florentine as well as the Englishman or the American—in a Roman restaurant: the restlessness, the waving of menus, the gradually mounting irritation that leaves the waiter completely unmoved. But when the stranger has become accustomed to this calm, it has its relaxing attractions.

The Roman restaurant is perhaps the last true inn or tavern in Europe, playing that welcoming multi-faced role that inns performed in the days of the horse-drawn coach. Europeans in general have tended to follow the Anglo-Saxon practice of setting up separate establishments for food and drink. On the one hand there is the bar, a leisurely invitation to get drunk, and on the other the restaurant, which chivvies the customer out on a conveyor-belt system. The Roman restaurateur is contemptuous of both barbarisms. His customers drink as well as eat, seated decorously at a table with carafe and glass. And if a patron wants to entertain his friends until the small hours, no one will question his right, least of all the restaurateur. He regards himself as a professional host. He leaves the cooking to experts— even if on occasion the expert is *mamma*—and he throws himself into the exhausting minutiae of making his customers welcome.

I got to know one of these *padroni* very well, making long trips across the city to the Campo dei Fiori to eat in his *trattoria*. "Marcello e Mario" was

Whatever his occupation or social station, a Roman prides himself on his style. Assuming a stance that would become an aristocrat in a palazzo drawing room, a neatly-groomed fruit barrow trader elegantly cocks his little finger as he pauses to take a glass of acqua minerale.

its self-explanatory name. Mario was the cook, a slow-moving man who would occasionally emerge from his pots and pans to stand looking solemnly at the square and then, as though reassured that it was still there, return to his cave. There was an old, inefficient man, Marcello's father, whose main contribution was to get in the way. And then there was our host, Marcello, still in his thirties, dark, wiry, seemingly tireless and inexhaustibly cheerful. There were perhaps 14 tables in his tiny *trattoria*, each one of which he served. I've seen him at the end of a three-hour lunchtime session, when every muscle in his body must have been groaning with fatigue, when his face was white and glistening with sweat, and still he smiled and joked and added up his figures in a *cadenza*. The price of a meal could vary considerably, for if he liked you, or felt unusually cheerful, he might round it down to the nearest 1,000 lire.

Above all he was efficient and intensely proud of his profession. On one occasion an aggressive stranger slouched in and demanded roast trout. He got it—served in the Roman manner in its full panoply of head, tail, fins and skin. The customer directed a torrent of abuse at the old man who had served him. Was this how they ate in Rome? Like dogs in a bone yard? If the establishment could not do its job properly and fillet the trout, could he at least have a fresh plate on which to deposit the unprintable detritus? The restaurant was crowded: Marcello seemed to be serving a dozen people at once. Yet still he found the time and the patience to hasten to his customer and, at his table, to fillet the trout for him, pacifying him in an undertone—a true professional at work.

Perhaps the establishment of "Marcello e Mario" may, in time, resemble the "Ristorante Pancrazio", which is only a stone's throw away, but it will need a lot of time. The "Pancrazio" is superior not only in size but in atmosphere as well. Pietro Macchione, owner of the "Pancrazio", is one of the Campo dei Fiori's aristocrats—he boasts of having been born there, not simply in Rome. So was his father. And his father's father. And his grandfather's father. He has a staff of waiters but still lives above the restaurant, still takes an active and loving part in it. He even boasts of having been thrown into prison for his restaurant's sake.

What happened is that Macchione was arrested for exploring, without a licence, a fragment of Rome's buried past. His restaurant occupies a part—a miniscule part—of the long-vanished Theatre of Pompey. The theatre, built in 55 B.C., was the largest, most sumptuous and the oldest of all the theatres of the ancient city. The section that touches Campo dei Fiori, and in whose foundations lies Macchione's restaurant, was the curved proscenium and stage. From here ran a famous arcade of one hundred huge columns. It was in one of the adjoining halls, where the Senate met on the Ides of March, that Caesar fell.

Presumably the foundations of the theatre survive in their entirety, but the archaeologists have always quailed at the prospect of demolishing the half-dozen churches and hundreds of houses that now cover the vast site. One of these buildings is the "Pancrazio". Soon after Macchione succeeded his father in 1944, he became curious about the ruins below his restaurant and began moling downwards into what were presumably the theatre's tunnels. He was promptly arrested on behalf of the indignant Superintendent of Antiquities. To be fair, Macchione's imprisonment was brief. He returned to his restaurant in triumph and resumed his career of restaurateur —and archaeologist: the Superintendent of Antiquities agreed to permit Macchione to dig further into the ground below the restaurant. Nearly 30 years later Macchione has uncovered an impressive area of the theatre, and as the theatre has emerged the restaurant has edged in until half of the excavations are occupied by the "Pancrazio".

But Macchione is very much a Roman in his refusal to make tourist bait of his discoveries. The "Ristorante Pancrazio" gives no indication of its fascinating interior; on the contrary, its entrance is almost forbidding. Located in the ominously named Grass Snake Street, the restaurant is marked by an ugly archway. At night the restaurant windows are hospitably lit, but the glass is opaque: the only other illumination is a glittering lamp over the arch. Any casual visitor hurrying through the tiny square and glimpsing that dark tunnel would be more likely to increase his speed than linger. But should his goal be the "Pancrazio", then he will find himself in another world. Although now nearly 15 feet below ground, the restaurant betrays no hint of subterranean claustrophobia. Macchione, who looks the epitome of an unimaginative businessman, has decorated his restaurant with the sensitivity of a stage designer. A few of the original columns have been replaced *in situ*, and there is a bust or two. The cold white wines are served in reproduction earthenware amphorae. All in all, it is a satisfying blend of traditionalism, independence and hospitality that makes the "Pancrazio", like so many other restaurants in the city, a subtle revelation, an instructive look into the character of Rome and the Roman.

Drama in the Streets

A market transaction is transformed into instant theatre as a housewife acts the part of a suspicious shopper and a fruit seller that of the unjustly accused.

Romans can convey as much meaning and emotion with faces, bodies and hands as with their spoken words—and often more. It is possible for two Romans to carry on a conversation across a street, in spite of impenetrable traffic noise, simply by gestures and grimaces. This ability to mime seems to be an innate gift: in the 16th Century, Italian comedy troupes played all over Europe to foreign audiences who, while they were unable to understand any of the lines, successfully followed the plots by watching the artful movements of the performers. On the pavements of Rome the acting tradition still flourishes. Italian writer Luigi Barzini has asserted that it is more important for a Roman child's survival to learn to read facial expressions than to learn to read print. And when speech and facial expression differ, Barzini suggests, forget the words—just believe the face.

It is no use turning one's back on a particularly lively discussion—the language of the hands goes on, and on.

Not even attempting to get a hand in edgewise, a listener placidly submits to a histrionic harangue from a lady friend who is quite unencumbered by her cane.

A marketwoman's hand says as emphatically as her lips "Guardate che freschezza"—"See how fresh!"

In a narrow Roman street a man uses body as well as hand language to give a vivid description of his own adventure on wheels to a couple of obliging listeners.

A traffic accident is a sure trigger for an explosion of rhetoric, and gestures to match. Even bystanders can soon get drawn into passionate participation.

To express the depth and multiplicity of his frustrations, a Roman traffic policeman has no need to resort to words. Face and outstretched arms say it all.

3

The Ancient Heart

Dominating the ancient heart of Rome is an enormous edifice of peroxide white marble—the Vittorio Emanuele Monument, constructed at the turn of the century to commemorate the unification of Italy in 1870. Boldly perched upon one of its many platforms is a 39-by-39-foot statue of the portly first king of Italy astride his equally portly charger (so large is the horse that after it was cast and before the king was put in place on it, the foundrymen held a celebration lunch in its belly). The king is peering up the Via del Corso to the north—the direction from which he came to assume the crown. The dazzling marble around and behind him is adorned with golden Victories clutching golden wreaths; columns soar pointlessly into the sky; steps ascend nowhere in particular. At one of the monument's many levels is the tomb of Italy's unknown soldier, at another the so-called Altar of the Nation. Within the monument are a barracks, two museums, a library and archives holding 350,000 documents. Romans have given up trying to explain or apologize for the preposterous structure. It does not even provide them with the wry amusement, the oblique pride, that Londoners derive from the pseudo-Gothic Albert Memorial or Parisians from the Eiffel Tower. At best they ignore it.

Francis Marion Crawford, the American novelist, saw it being built in 1905. "When in a future century, the broad flood of patriotism shall have subsided within the straight riverbed of sober history," he predicted, "men will wonder why Victor Emmanuel, honest and brave though he was, received the greater share of praise, and Cavour and Garibaldi the less." The choice seems even more eccentric now that the monarchy Vittorio Emanuele founded has gone to the great rubbish heap of Italy's discarded political systems. But although the memorial's "wedding cake" architecture is deplorable, its siting beside the Capitol is appropriate. For it is right and proper that the unification of Italy should be recorded close to the spot that has witnessed the greatest triumphs and disasters of Rome's long history.

It is the steep Capitoline Hill, together with the Palatine Hill to the south and the Valley of the Forum between them, that encompasses what most people mean when they say "Rome". The three landmarks form a rectangle perhaps half a mile long and a quarter of a mile wide, yet this small area, no larger than a city park, has had more effect on the history of Europe—and hence of the world—than entire countries. This is where Rome was born more than 2,500 years ago. Every square foot of it has yielded something significant, and within it there is no building, no ruin, whose details have not been minutely recorded.

The lugubrious face of the Bocca della Verità ("Mouth of Truth"), once an ancient drainhole cover, now stands as a decoration outside a medieval church, S. Maria in Cosmedin. A belief persists from the Middle Ages that if anyone puts a hand into its mouth and tells a lie, Truth will respond by biting the hand.

I intended to explore it as a unit. First I would climb to the Capitol, the religious citadel of ancient Rome, then descend into the Forum, where the city's daily life was lived; and finally ascend again to the imperial Palatine Hill, which still holds the great substructures of the palaces of the Caesars. I thought this journey might take a day. Instead it took several days, and at the end I had glimpsed—if only fleetingly—the richly variegated history of ancient Rome.

About the year 800 B.C. the axis of what was to become Rome was a craggy, wooded hilltop set in a circle of others with a marsh below and populated by a few shepherds. Over the next century or so settlers from the surrounding country made their way to the crests of these hills, seeking coolness and safety. The Latins, as one tribe was called, are supposed to have settled on the Palatine Hill, the steep landmark that stands in the centre of the others like the hub of a wheel, while another tribe, the Sabines, built their huts on the Esquiline Hill half a mile to the north-east.

At first the villagers fought among themselves, but by 700 B.C. their expanding populations began to coalesce. In time the uninhabited Capitoline Hill became a religious centre and fortress; and so Rome began. But posterity would demand a more dramatic explanation for the moment when a group of villages united to become a city. Posterity found it in the story of Romulus, the legendary founder of Rome who as an infant had been tossed with his twin brother Remus into the Tiber and rescued by a female wolf that then saved the boys from starvation by suckling them. According to the legend, Romulus in 753 B.C. ordered the building of a great wall around the Palatine Hill and thus created the city to which he gave his name. The wall—which was supposed to protect the citizens from evil as well as enemies—was constructed along lines laid down by the Etruscans, the first builders of cities in Italy, and it grew to encompass the Capitol. "And all the nobles of the earth, together with their wives and children, came to live in this new city of Rome", stated a 10th-Century guide book, *The Description of the Golden City*. But it is more likely that these newcomers were escaped slaves and criminals seeking the safety of the Asylum that Romulus established on the Capitoline Hill.

To the present day part of the Capitol remains bare where a sombre cliff rises 60 feet high. This is the Tarpeian Rock, and it enters history with a story that is typically blood-soaked and typically Roman in its bleak approval of immediate vengeance upon a citizen who had harmed the state. The Sabines were besieging the Capitol when Tarpeia, a priestess of Vesta, the Goddess of the Hearth, descended from the hill to fetch water from a sacred fountain in the place that would one day be known as the Forum. It was thronged with the enemy but they revered Vesta as much as did the Latins, and they let the girl through. During the chaffing conversation between the pretty girl and the bored Sabine warriors, she was persuaded to betray the citadel by opening the gate at night. Her price? "What

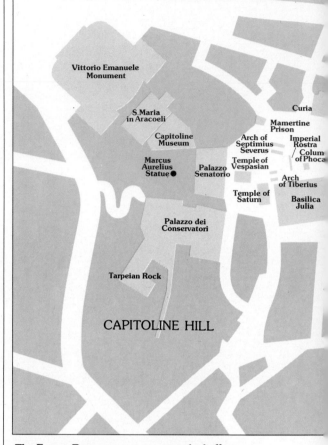

The Forum Romanum, once a marshy hollow between the Capitoline and Palatine Hills, has been left by the passing centuries crowded with ruins of buildings of both Republican and Imperial periods. In this diagrammatic map the main monuments are identified and located together with some of the important buildings of later eras clustered in the vicinity.

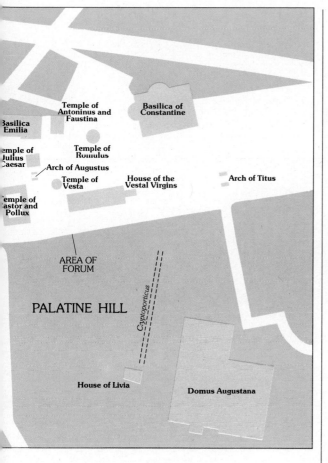

you wear upon your left arm", she said, not knowing the word for the gold bracelet that each man wore. She opened the gate that night, but as each Sabine warrior passed, he paid the debt instead by throwing down upon her the heavy shield that he also carried over his left arm.

Tarpeia's death marked the beginning of the violence that still taints this cliff. Traitors to imperial Rome were hurled from the rock, and throughout the Middle Ages the gardens that now occupy the spot were the execution site for all Rome, Here stood the gallows with their rotting corpses in full sight of the city; here were the machines for decapitation, for disembowelling, stretching, cracking, ripping—all the ingenious devices for sending a human being out of the world in the greatest shame and agony. Eventually the executioners took their trade to the riverside, by the bridge of Sant'Angelo, but they left behind them, deep in the Capitoline Hill, another grim reminder of the dark side of Rome—the Mamertine prison.

The prison is a chapel now, consecrated to St. Peter who supposedly was imprisoned here by Nero. Notice boards urge the faithful to visit it, and the approaches have that fairground touch that is never far from Rome's pious monuments. But as you pass through the little church and begin the descent to the cells, the cheerful 20th-Century vulgarity is replaced by an atmosphere that is almost pure evil.

The dungeons lie one above the other and are now connected by a staircase that was built to allow pilgrims to descend to the so-called Apostle's cell. Constructed of enormous blocks of stone, the prison is perhaps the oldest structure in Rome. What was it in the beginning? A well? A tomb? No one knows. Whatever its original function it became a prison during the Republic (509 to 27 B.C.) and was an affront even to many Romans: the historian Sallust described it as a place "enclosed on all sides by walls, and above it is a chamber with a vaulted roof of stone. Neglect, darkness and stench make it hideous and fearsome to behold." But it was the visiting Englishman Charles Dickens who best captured its atmosphere. "The dread and gloom of the ponderous, obdurate old prison . . . come up as in a dark mist through the floor. . . . It is all so silent and so close, and tomb like . . . so black and stealthy, and stagnant, and naked."

The roll-call of the slain, whose bodies were dragged up from the prison with hooks and thrown into the great sewer, the Cloaca Maxima, is a long and chilling one. Sejanus, the treacherous minister of Tiberius, was slaughtered here, and so was the sadistic Jugurtha, ruler of Numidia in North Africa. The great Vercingetorix, who led an uprising of Gauls that nearly defeated Julius Caesar, and Simon Bar Gioras, the gallant defender of Jerusalem, met ignominious deaths here as well. The prison was well situated to receive such enemies of the state. It lay beside the processional route that the victorious generals took on their way to the great Temple of Jupiter on the Capitoline Hill; and the captive commander who had been exhibited in chains during the triumphal march was thrown into the

Baroque angels line the bridge leading over the Tiber to the Castel Sant'Angelo. Built as Hadrian's tomb, the castle became a papal fort in medieval times.

Mamertine before the procession wound up the slope to the Temple.

The Temple of Jupiter, high on its hill, figured as the centre of the pagan Roman religion for nearly 800 years, ever since its dedication in 509 B.C. Again and again it was rebuilt, growing ever larger and more magnificent until its zenith under the mad young emperor Domitian in the 1st Century A.D. Inside was a gigantic figure of Jupiter, copied from a statue by the Greek sculptor Phidias and covered with a combination of gold and ivory that went by the splendid name of chryselephantine. Outside all was dazzling marble and gold. The very roof was gilded, and Rome came to be known as the "Golden City" from this glittering glory on the southern crest of the Capitoline Hill.

It was with relief that I left the Mamertine prison and trudged up the road that had led to the now-vanished temple and looked across to the northern crest of the Capitol where another temple, that of Jupiter's consort, Juno Moneta, had stood. The mint was built here, under the protection of the goddess from whose name many European languages were to take their word for money. Here, too, stood the cages of sacred geese whose furious cackling on a night in 390 B.C. warned the citizens that a besieging force of Gauls was climbing the hill. Every year afterwards the Romans celebrated their salvation by carrying a goose in a thanksgiving procession—and by ritually crucifying a dog, because the dogs of the citadel had failed to bark an alarm on that night.

During the long darkness that fell on Rome after the barbarian invasion of the 4th and 5th Centuries A.D., the temples of Juno and of Jupiter vanished. The aqueducts that had supplied imperial Rome fell into disrepair, so the high ground was deserted, including the Capitoline Hill. The population fell from an estimated one million in the 2nd Century A.D. to 17,000 in the 13th Century. In the Middle Ages the Capitol became known as the Monte Caprino, the Hill of Goats. Yet the impoverished inhabitants of the city never forgot its former glory, and regarded it as a sacred spot haunted by ghosts from an age of vanished greatness.

They believed that deep within the hill, in a vast subterranean hall, an everlasting feast was attended by the heroes of Roman history. Legend tells of a bold explorer finding his way into the hall and at first being awed by the terrible, still company. Then he tried to steal a jewel from one of the diner's necks, and the whole assembly came to glaring life. Here, too, was supposed to hang the magic mirror for the emperors to see whatever was happening in their realm. Near the Temple of Jupiter, it was claimed, stood the marvel known as Rome's Salvation—a gallery of golden statues, each with a bell round its neck, and each representing a province. When a bell rang, the lords of Rome knew in which province rebellion was taking place.

Today the southern face of the Capitoline Hill gives the appearance of an elaborate stage setting, with its piled-up ruins. But the northern side presents quite another appearance. It was laid out in Renaissance times

A Pageant of Emperors, Popes and Kings

B.C. 753	Traditional date of the foundation of Rome
509	Republic of Rome founded
390	Sack of Rome by the Gauls. The Capitol saved from occupation by the warning cackle of sacred geese. Servian Wall constructed around Rome
312	Appian Way completed as far as Capua by the Censor Appius Claudius
241	End of First Punic War with the Roman victory over Carthage
216	Defeat of the Romans by Hannibal at the Battle of Cannae in Second Punic War
146	Destruction of Carthage and end of Third Punic War
142	Completion of the Pons Æmilius, the first stone bridge over the Tiber
c. 78	Tabularium built on the Capitol to house the state archives
55	Opening of the Theatre of Pompey, Rome's first stone-built theatre
44	Murder of Caesar
c. 27	Foundation of the Roman Empire under Augustus
A.D. c. 64	Martyrdom of St Peter in the Circus of Nero. Great fire of Rome
c. 67	Martyrdom of St Paul in Rome
70	Sack of Jerusalem by Titus
135	Castel Sant'Angelo begun by Hadrian
176	Column of Marcus Aurelius erected after his victories over the Germans and Sarmatians
203	Arch of Septimius Severus erected to celebrate the victories of Severus and his sons Caracalla and Geta in Assyria
271	The Seven Hills of Rome enclosed by the Aurelian Wall
284	Division of the Empire into the Western and Eastern Empires under Diocletian
330	Capital of the Empire transferred by Constantine the Great to Byzantium
410	Sack of Rome by Alaric the Goth
440	Leo the Great becomes Pope
476	End of the Western Empire

along grandiose lines, and remains one of the great urban set pieces of the world in spite of the overbearing presence now of the near-by Vittorio Emanuele Monument. As I climbed the broad ramp that leads to the Piazza del Campidoglio (*Campidoglio* is merely the Italian for the Latin *Capitolium*), I had an impression not so much of architecture as of sculpture, with palaces, fountains, statues, steps, trees and shrubs combined in a single harmony. I paused at the top of the ramp between two enormous statues of Castor and Pollux. Beyond them stretched the Piazza del Campidoglio in its full harmonious beauty. It was designed by Michelangelo in the second golden age of Rome—the height of the Renaissance when, after a thousand years of decline, the city was gradually transformed under a succession of ambitious popes. Although Michelangelo designed the piazza and surrounding buildings, their construction was not undertaken until after his death; but his concept was powerful enough to ensure that his scheme would be realized by those whose job it was to execute it.

At the centre of the piazza stands the bronze equestrian statue of the emperor Marcus Aurelius. The statue has a curious history. It survived the fury of early Christian bigots only because they thought it represented the first Christian emperor, Constantine. For centuries it stood close to the Church of St. John Lateran, "Rome's Cathedral". The statue was always a famous and central landmark in Rome. A pope hanged a rebellious city prefect by his hair from the horse in 955; and in the 14th Century, a self-styled tribune of Rome, Cola di Rienzo, celebrated his rise to power by having the bronze horse converted into a fountain that poured wine from one nostril and water from the other.

When in the 16th Century Michelangelo was seeking a focal point for his piazza, his gaze fell upon the beautiful statue of the mounted emperor, still glittering with gilt, His patron, Pope Paul III, was as eager as Michelangelo to have the work removed to the Capitol. But the Canons of St. John Lateran were reluctant to part with it, and only a combination of threats and cajolery persuaded them.

Michelangelo personally supervised the placement of this most famous of Rome's statues, making it look as natural, as inevitable on its spot as the great dome is the natural crown for St. Peter's. Indeed, he is supposed to have been so satisfied by its effect that once it had been lifted on to its base, he stepped up to the emperor's horse and gave it the command to walk.

The emperor astride the horse is calm and dignified, He is riding bareback, his sandalled feet balancing him comfortably, his hand raised in an imperial but friendly salute. The clothes he wears are without adornment or sign of his high office. The expression of the firm, intelligent face is rather remote. It is the face of a man who could not only detach himself from affairs of state to write his "Meditations", but also of a man who could ignore the rumours of his wife's unfaithfulness and instead raise a statue to her chastity. There are still traces of gilding to be seen on the statue.

In a shadowy alley near the sunlit church of S. Nicola in Carcere, a group of cats lounge about after dining on spaghetti provided by a faithful well-wisher.

A City of Cats

Teeming tribes of cats haunt many areas of Rome—the Forum, the Colosseum, the Theatre of Marcellus and other enclaves of the ancient world. They are descendants of a flourishing feline population that was commented on by writers as early as the 5th Century B.C. Imported to Rome from cat-worshipping Egypt, they have survived from age to age, proceeding in haughty detachment from the affairs of the humans sharing the city with them. Nowadays, living in the peace of government-protected ruins, fed by people who make it their business to offer them a regular tribute of food (including *pasta*), they act as if the city were indeed their undisputed inheritance.

Staring disdainfully, a cat rests by a column.

When they disappear, runs one of the city's countless prophecies of doom, Rome will perish.

Behind the statue, at the far end of the square, rises the graceful façade of the Palazzo Senatorio. Also designed by Michelangelo, it houses a medieval structure built for the 56 senators who were elected after a popular uprising in 1143. But the history of the site goes back further than that. Its base is set firmly on the massive blocks of the Tabularium, constructed around 78 B.C. to house the archives of imperial Rome. The palace is used today by the city's civil servants, including the mayor, whose office is here. At 8 o'clock each morning local government officers stream into the building just as their predecessors 2,000 years ago streamed into the Tabularium. The link with Rome's past is recognized officially, too. The city celebrates its birthday on April 21 each year in the piazza in front of the palace—the same day on which Romulus in 753 B.C. was supposed to have laid out Rome's boundaries.

On opposite sides of the piazza are two beautiful buildings that are now used as museums. But they are not museums as the world generally knows them—places where dead things are ranged in rows before wearying eyes. I found that for all their noble exteriors, these museums were intimate inside: more like the glass-fronted cabinets in which families display their sentimental treasures. For once I was not irritated by the Roman reluctance to describe or sometimes even to label. The feeling came over me that the museums were private places maintained by Romans for their own household goods, and that I was here only on sufferance.

This sensation was strongest among the sculptures in the Capitoline Museum—the oldest public art collection in the world, started in 1471 by Pope Sixtus IV—particularly in the dark gallery that houses the portrait busts of emperors and patricians. I found myself staring, almost hypnotized, into each marble face, trying to relate it to the long-dead face of flesh and blood, and to that other visage that history conjures in the mind. The hatchet-faced, high-civil-servant expression of the young emperor Augustus; the chubby, amicable good looks of the young Nero; the bull-like strength of Caracalla; the sodden bestiality of Vitellius—they seem merely to deepen the mystery of what these men were really like.

But one thing emerged with appalling clarity, and that was the ferocity of life during Rome's imperial age. These exhibits did have identifying labels, and the check list of exhibits reads like a dirge of decadence:

No. 42 Lucilla, daughter of Marcus Aurelius: put to death by her husband.
No. 43 Commodus, Emperor: murdered.
No. 44 Crispina, wife of Commodus: murdered.
No. 45 Pertinax, Emperor for three months: murdered.
No. 46 Didius Julianus, successor to Pertinax: murdered.
No. 51 Geta, brother of Caracalla and murdered by him.

Zigzagging bricks protrude from the core of an ancient wall whose masonry has been stripped away. Although generations of Romans have plundered such walls for their marble facings, the inner walls often survive—testament to the building skills of the early Romans.

The terrible list goes on. Natural death for emperors and their immediate male relatives was almost unknown in the latter years of the Empire. Again and again murderer was murdered, and I suddenly understood why the emperor Commodus, who was assassinated in A.D. 192 had the walls of his palace faced with marble which was so highly polished that it acted as a mirror in which he could see when his enemies were approaching—a kind of advance warning system.

As I left the museum I wondered what these men were trying to purchase at such a fearful price. Political dominance? Hardly, when their high office depended upon the whims of a garrison of roughneck soldiers. Sensual gratification? They could enjoy that as private citizens without the constant fear of meeting a violent death. The simple answer, perhaps, is greed for personal power; but that could only be exercised in the knowledge that it might end with a dagger thrust from a slave.

It was in the museum on the opposite side of the piazza—the Palazzo dei Conservatori—that I found the link between Rome's past and present strongest. Here continuity is made explicit. The building itself stands on the site of the Temple of Jupiter. The ancient tablets inside listing the city fathers have been painstakingly restored and brought up to date, so that they give the entire succession of officers from Roman times to today. Here, too, is the bust of Lucius Junius Brutus, the founder of the Republic, that sums up both the nobility and the brutality of the Roman character: dauntless fortitude balanced by narrow arrogance, a rigid adherence to a pattern of right conduct balanced by a total lack of imagination. Looking at that face I understood not only how the majesty of Roman Law came into being, but also how the savage Colosseum games could be tolerated.

Not far from the marble bust of Brutus, I came upon the most famous of the city's symbols: the figure of the she-wolf that suckled Romulus and Remus. With wild eyes and bared teeth, she seems to be protecting them from all harm. Was this the famous statue that once stood in a small shrine at the foot of the Palatine Hill? It is possible. Cicero remarked that the figure had been struck by lightning and I noticed a jagged fracture in the hindquarters that could have been caused by great heat. The plump figures of the twins were added in the 15th Century—an addition lamented by purists but typical of the Roman habit of putting saints on the columns of pagan emperors and turning temples into churches. The statue is a much-loved symbol, but the Romans do not hesitate to make fun of it. A popular poster shows one of the twins spitting out the milk in disgust at the taste.

My next goal was the Forum, but before I took on so ambitious a project I allowed myself to be drawn back to the Campidoglio. I had paused to enjoy the sight of the piazza in front of the Palazzo Senatoria when I spotted a youth marching briskly across the piazza towards me. His shabby clothes and battered rucksack were incongruous in the marble elegance of the Campidoglio. His hair, bleached white by the sun, and his tanned skin

Filled with golden light and dwarfing the symphony orchestra performing under its vaulted roof, the ruined Basilica of Maxentius in the Forum emphasizes the majestic scale of late imperial buildings. Begun about A.D. 308 by the emperor Maxentius and completed by Constantine after 312, it served originally as a law court and exchange.

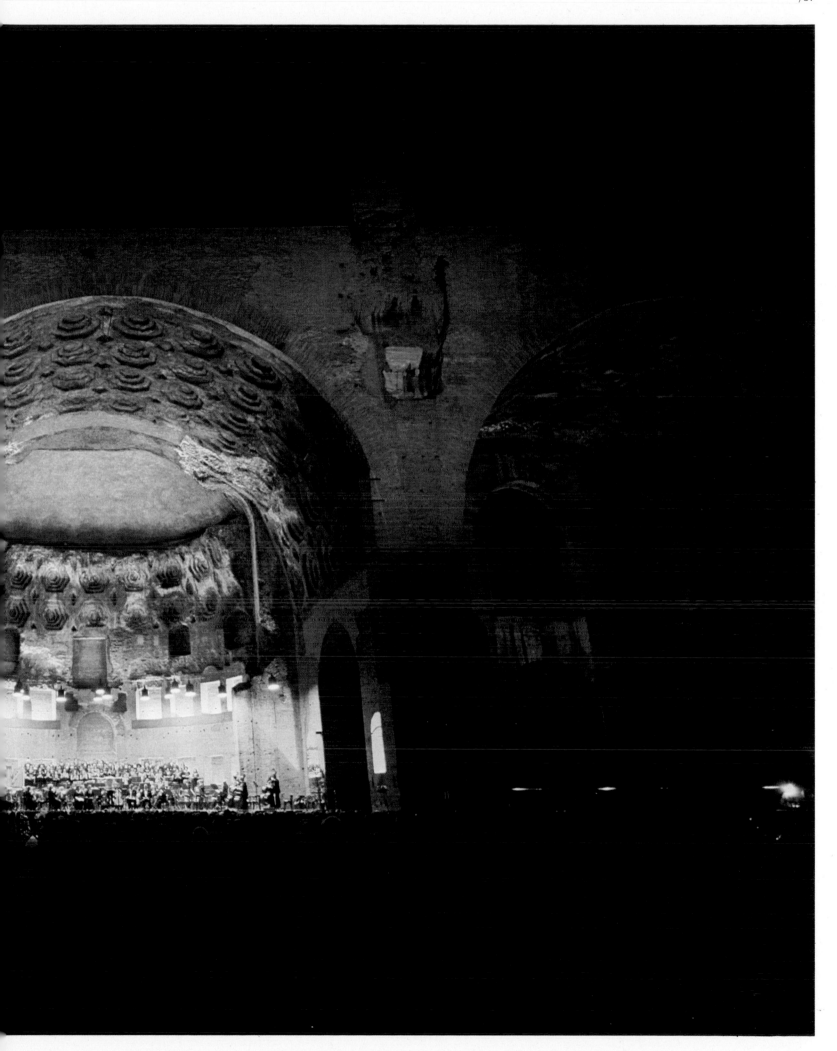

proclaimed him instantly as one of those young people who spend their summer travelling down the entire length of Italy. He strode up to a near-by fountain in his heavy boots, engaged in a vigorous and illegal toilet in the cool green water, splashed me generously, apologized and demanded, "Where's the Forum?"

I told him that it was close by, and we fell to talking. A cheerful young German lad, he had arrived in Rome just an hour before and was un-abashedly "doing" the city in eight hours flat before leaving for Naples in the cool of the evening. He had homed in on the Capitol as a natural starting point for a quick tour of Rome. I explained that the Forum was the next stage of my journey back through time, so together we went over to the flight of steps that flow down the south face of the Capitoline Hill towards the entrance to the Forum.

Seen from this height, the great *Forum Romanum* displays a kind of unity that evaporates once you find yourself actually wandering among its tumbled stones. Forming a long rectangle, it slopes slightly upward towards the mass of the Palatine Hill. The view—so often reproduced in history and travel books—is familiar. There they all are: the massive tri-umphal arch of Septimius Severus, the ruins of the Temple of Saturn, the single column of Phocas, the three columns of Castor and Pollux, and, in the distance, the Arch of Titus, commemorating his capture of Jerusalem in A.D. 70. Yet in spite of its familiarity, it is still a stirring sight. Even the most ebullient coach-loads of tourists tend to fall silent on first glimpse of the vista. So did my German friend. Over the next ten minutes he looked his fill, asking only an occasional question. Then he heaved up his rucksack. "Aren't you coming down?" I enquired. "No," he replied. "I'd rather leave it like that." And with a casual wave, he was off, clumping across the square in his thick-soled boots.

Probably he was right. The Forum must be one of the most bewildering archaeological sites in the world. The level of sheer destruction is in itself quite extraordinary. Some of this is a direct result of ancient strife. But most occurred long after the fall of imperial Rome, during the Middle Ages and Renaissance when builders, greedy for materials with which to construct new churches, palaces and monuments, ransacked the place. And what the barbarians and builders left, the archaeologists dug out and picked over, leaving behind a littered boneyard.

The Forum, therefore, is one of the few places where a guide really is necessary for the short-term visitor. The fortunate person with time to spare can return repeatedly—always armed with guide-books. Here is a true democracy of ignorance: one is just as likely to spot professors con-fusedly glancing between books and object described, as to see visiting secretaries and businessmen in the same predicament and in a similar state of bewilderment. Viewed from above, these figures, their noses buried in their fat little books, resemble priests reading their breviaries.

But they are right to persist. The only effective technique for exploring the Forum is to drift and peer and read and drift again, and time is essential for that. In this, the authorities are generous: instead of closing for the three-hour Roman "lunch hour", the Forum and Palatine remain open until dusk; and for a ludicrously low entrance fee the visitor can spend nearly 11 hours exploring both. The unshaded northern section of the Forum is best tackled in the cool of morning; then, as the sun mounts overhead, you can retreat up the hill and take shelter among the trees and fountains of the Palatine. There are rules forbidding the eating of alfresco meals—a reasonable prohibition considering the dismal tons of rubbish that fall to the Roman streets every day. But the Forum and Palatine custodians are a philosophical, detached breed, little disposed to harry people, and the person with a packed lunch can usually count on eating it in peace. There are not many things better than bread and cheese and wine consumed under an *ilex* on the Palatine.

I had all day before me; and so, while applauding the young German's strong-minded refusal to become bogged down by detail, I began my descent into the Forum—down the steps, through the phalanx of ice-cream vans and souvenir stalls on the street below, and so to the modest little ticket office where a few lire bought me a ticket to the past.

It was not until the 19th Century that the first systematic excavation of the long-buried Forum began. For centuries it had been known only as the *Campo Vaccino*, the Cow Field, a place where cattle were pastured. Enough ruins remained to suggest that this was a place out of the ordinary, but after it had ceased to be a quarry for ready-made stone it held no interest for anyone. Once archaeologists had unearthed the first of the Forum's treasures, however, the pace of excavation quickened, and was accelerated by the nationalist fervour of the late 19th Century and the 1930s. There cannot now be a single stone in the Forum that has not been exposed, measured, photographed and catalogued. And in the process the trees that appeared in those elegant views of the Forum recorded by 18th- or 19th-Century artists have been felled, depriving the area of shade.

The archaeologists cannot be blamed entirely for this. Their job has never been an easy one. The Forum is composed of layer upon layer of ruins and it must be difficult for the scientist to decide whether to stop his excavation at this Renaissance palace or that Imperial floor, or at the prehistoric tomb that lies beneath them both. What is inexcusable, however, is that the city fathers, who have permitted their Forum to be dissected in the name of scholarship, provide no reconstruction of the jumbled remains. There is a superb model of classical Rome, but instead of being displayed here, where it would be of value, it is housed, through a quirk of bureaucratic logic, some three miles away.

In such a chaos of ruins and centuries it is easy to give up in despair. So I decided to begin at the beginning, chronologically, and went to stand by the single block of stone which is all that remains of the Shrine of Vulcan. Here, according to tradition, the Sabine and Latin tribes that populated the hills of Rome first came to terms in the 7th Century B.C.; and the Forum, which before had been little more than a marsh between the Capitol and the Palatine, was established as a communal market place.

But in the days of its glory, during the early Christian era, the Forum ceased to be a market and became instead a showpiece, in which enormous ceremonial buildings jostled for space. Half a dozen temples, two vast public halls, three triumphal arches, the spacious house of the Vestal Virgins and a liberal sprinkling of honorary columns and statues were all crammed in and around an area little bigger than Trafalgar Square or Times Square. Two of the great arches survive—probably because they were used as parts of fortification in the Middle Ages. To the left of the Shrine of Vulcan looms the triumphal Arch of Septimius Severus, built in A.D. 203 to celebrate the victories of the emperor Severus and his sons, Caracalla and Geta, over the Parthians, Arabs, and Adjabeni, inhabitants of ancient Syria. Geta's name no longer appears in the inscription on the arch. It was erased on the orders of Caracalla, who murdered him nine years after the arch was erected. Such triumphal arches—there are three still standing in Rome—have had an enduring influence: Marble Arch in London and the Arc de Triomphe in Paris are only two of the many replicas of the Arch of Septimius Severus.

I passed under the arch and was confronted at the other side by the remains of the New Rostra, the platform on which Roman orators addressed the populace. It was used by Cicero, Rome's greatest public speaker. Here, too, Mark Antony made his immortal speech after the murder of Caesar. "He mounted the Rostra", wrote the historian Plutarch, pronounced the customary eulogy for the dead dictator—then "when he saw that the multitude was moved by his words, changed his tone to one of compassion, and taking the robe of Caesar, all bloody as it was, unfolded it to view, pointing out the many places in which it had been pierced and Caesar wounded". It was a masterly manoeuvre and, as Plutarch laconically remarked, "All further orderly procedure was at an end, of course."

Of all the splendid public buildings that once crowded the Forum, only one remains intact—the Curia or Senate House. Now stripped of its marble façade, it is no more than an ugly red brick box. But inside it preserves an austere dignity in keeping with its function as the seat of government in Republican Rome. The Senate in these early years excited an almost religious awe. But by the 1st Century A.D., when Rome was already ruled by emperors, the power of the Senate had become illusory. As the Roman historian Tacitus complained, the senators "must show neither satisfaction at the death of one emperor, nor gloom at the accession of another: so their features were carefully arranged in a blend of tears and smiles, mourning and flattery". In fact, on imperial orders, the

Forgotten Games

When the marble floor of the Basilica Julia in the Roman Forum was laid bare by excavation, more than a hundred *tabulae lusoriae*—gaming boards—were discovered, carved into the paving stones. The great basilica, begun by Julius Caesar and completed by Augustus, was used as a civil law court, and was always full of idlers gambling away the intervals between court cases. Although such sport was supposedly illegal in public places, except during the festival of the Saturnalia, it evidently was tolerated here.

The Romans—including even their emperors—were passionate gamblers, and ancient accounts mention some of the board games they played, although failing to give the precise rules. One, called "soldiers", was played on a squared board (top right) and may have resembled draughts; others suggest possible rules by their layout. But for most of them every clue has vanished.

On this board gamblers played according to long-forgotten rules.

The game played on this square was probably more like draughts than chess.

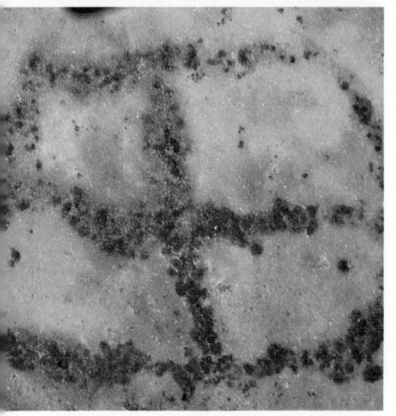

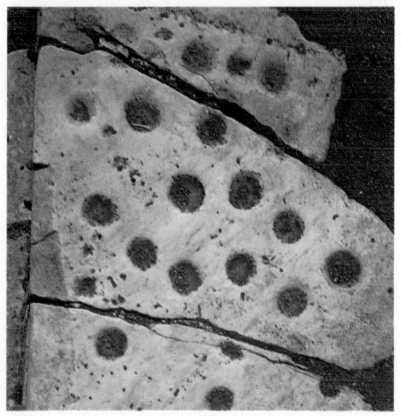

A scratched pattern on a marble flagstone remains; the game is lost.

Gamblers apparently bet on which hole would stop their rolled marbles.

Senate was burned down frequently. The structure that stands on the site today dates from A.D. 283.

Inside the Curia is a battered pedestal on which once stood a golden statue of the goddess Victory. This figure became the object of a tug-of-war between the pagans and the Christians during the reign of Constantine, the first Christian emperor, and continued to be an issue for many years to come as the Romans remained divided in their religious loyalties. The pagans put up a stout fight to keep their statue, while the Christians wanted it removed; so the statue appeared and disappeared according to the religious bias of each emperor. Early in the 5th Century the Christians won the battle: the statue was expelled, and, in fact, the Curia became a church. So it was preserved when all else in the Forum was being dismantled.

All around the Curia lie naked ruins. This shadeless expanse of broken stone would be oppressive were it not interrupted by a delightful copse where grow the three sacred plants of Mediterranean civilization: the grapevine, the fig and the olive. Near by, towards the Palatine, aesthetics, humanity and the demands of scholarship have provided yet another delight: three lovely pools in the ruins of the House of the Vestals, filled once again with water. The panting groups of tourists always slow up here to gaze hypnotized at the gleaming surface and darting goldfish, swish a hand through the coolness, or sit on the marble slabs beneath the headless statues of the Vestals standing in a row.

Although Christian propaganda turned most of the pagan gods into demons, it had no effect on the reputation of the Vestal Virgins. Reverence for them has come down through the centuries. Their task was vital: to tend the sacred flame in the small and graceful Temple of Vesta, the remains of which stand in the Forum under the slope of the Palatine. Vesta was the goddess of the hearth, and her temple here is a reminder that behind the pomp and majesty of Rome, its citizens were home-lovers. These people who conquered half the known world, whose legions marched from the deserts of Africa to the mists of Britain, looked upon exile as a form of living death; and in lonely garrisons in foreign lands they raised the concept of hearth and home to the status of a divinity.

The goddess Vesta is a vague and shadowy being, with few of the human ways of her fellow Roman deities. The worship of fire came down from remotest antiquity, and it is significant that Vesta's temple in the Forum was built in the shape of the rude huts that were the first buildings on the hills of Rome. The worship of her lingered on into the Christian era. Indeed, it can hardly be said to have ceased even now—on Easter Saturday in every Roman Catholic Church a fire is lit with flint and carried into the building to rekindle the dead candles.

The circular temple must have been a beautiful little building, with its graceful girdle of 20 columns. There was a hole in the roof, as there would have been in the primitive hut on which it was modelled, for smoke from

A popular emblem for centuries, the wolf that suckled Romulus, the city's mythical founder, and his twin Remus, is to be seen everywhere in Rome: right, an early stone copy of the famous classical bronze now in the Capitoline Museum; below, a sticker on a car's rear window.

the sacred fire to escape. Inside the shrine were kept wheat and salt—symbols of the state's resources—with other ancient and sacred objects.

The Vestals tended the fire on a rota basis of eight hours each; any guardian who let the sacred flame go out—and there were a few—was scourged in the darkness by the chief priest. During the Imperial period there were six members of the order, each chosen between the age of six and ten from among 20 pre-selected candidates. Each Vestal was enrolled for a period of 30 years, and at the end of her service was free to marry. But often a Vestal would renew her vows, for her position was highly esteemed. Vestals took precedence over every other woman except the empress, and shared with her the privilege of travelling in a wheeled vehicle in the city. Their reputation for sanctity and commonsense often led to their serving as mediators in quarrels, and they were entrusted with the custody of both public and private deeds and of wills. At banquets and at the Colosseum games they sat with the Imperial Family. A Vestal even had the power to pardon any condemned prisoner who crossed her path.

A Vestal lived by strict rules that went even beyond piety. In 420 B.C. a Vestal named Postumia incurred the wrath of the Sacred Order because of her style of dress and her sense of humour. According to the historian Livy, Postumia "was tried for incest, a crime of which she was not guilty, but suspicion had been raised by the fact that she was always got up prettily, and she had a wit which was a little too loose for a Virgin. After an adjournment she was found Not Guilty. Delivering judgment on behalf of the Board of Priests, the Chief Priest told her to stop making jokes and, in her dress and appearance, to aim at looking holy rather than smart".

The sternest punishment was reserved for the worst sin: breaking the vow of chastity. Those found guilty were buried alive. Pliny describes one such execution although this woman also was innocent. She was Cornelia, the Chief Vestal during the reign of the emperor Domitian, who seems to have condemned her on a vicious whim. "When she was being led down to the dreadful pit and her dress caught as she was being lowered, she turned and readjusted it and when the executioner offered her his hand, she declined it and drew back as though she put away with horror the idea of her chaste and pure body being defiled by his loathsome touch. Thus she preserved her sanctity to the last, and displayed all the tokens of a chaste woman, like Hecuba, truly."

Beyond the ruined temple of the Vestals lies the Palatine, and I headed for it. The Capitol and the Forum were now behind me, as I climbed towards the ancient city's seat of power: the palaces of the emperors. I walked up the hill past ruins shaded by trees, and became conscious of a deep melancholy that pervaded the place. Here, said a 12th-Century author, was the "palace of the Monarchy of the Earth, wherein is the capital seat of the whole world". This was the hill where dwelt monarchs who in their times ruled civilization; and its Latin name, *Palatium*, gave

birth to the word "palace". Here among the remains of the imperial dwell-
ings—the shattered hulks of brick, covered in creepers—it is virtually
impossible to avoid thoughts of *sic transit gloria mundi*, any more than
Byron could when he wandered over the Palatine:

Cypress and ivy, weed and wallflower grown
Matted and massed together, hillocks heaped
On what were chambers, arch crushed, column strown
In fragments, choked up vaults and frescoes steeped
In subterranean damps, where the owl peeped
Deeming it midnight . . .

And who lived where in these now-ruined halls? Compared with the
Palatine, the Forum is a model of clarity. Large areas of the hill have been
closed to the public since the Second World War, and there has been little
attempt to signpost the rest. With the best will in the world, it is impossible
to provide an adequate guide to the place, because most of its heritage has
been destroyed or jumbled, from the founding of the Roman Republic in
509 B.C. to the 16th Century A.D. when great Roman families laid out
pleasure gardens on the hill. Building succeeded building. Architect succeeded architect, and each destroyed what his predecessors had created.
By the time their work had come to an end, the Palatine was heaped with
rubble. Theodore Dwight, an American traveller and writer who visited the
Palatine Hill during the first wave of excavations in 1821, described it:
"The soil had at first the appearance of being thickly scattered with
gravel; but this proved to be owing to vast quantities of bricks, marble,
stones and pottery, broken into small bits and mingled by a long course
of cultivation. It seemed no very incredible thing, when we reflected what
piles of buildings had in former ages occupied the grounds . . . Here one
naturally thinks of subterranean apartments, and undiscovered treasures
hid beneath the ground; for in a place so teeming with memorials of
former times, a stranger thinks he could not rest until the dark interior is
exposed to view; and quite unsatisfied with what he sees upon the surface,
he feels that he would gladly lend his strength to lay open the foundations
of the immortal *Mons Palatinus.*"

That is exactly what has been going on for a century and more. The
hanging Farnese Gardens, for example, with which a 16th-Century cardinal, Alessandro Farnese, clothed the cliffs, must once have rivalled those
of Babylon; now most have been destroyed, victims of archaeological
exploration. On the crest of the Palatine itself enough remains of this
lovely creation to remind us of the price paid for such knowledge.

Gingerly making my way across temporary bridges that span man-made
chasms of brick, I climbed to the north slope of the hill. Here an underground tunnel built by Nero still maintains something of mystery and
beauty. It once formed part of his Golden House, a vast palace complex,
some of whose walls were encrusted with gems and pearls. When Nero

moved into his sumptuous new home, he exulted: "At last I am lodged like a man." His tenancy was short, however: four years after the palace was erected, Rome erupted in civil revolt, and Nero cut his throat in despair. Shadowy, cool, with the remains of elegant stucco decorations partially intact, the tunnel once allowed residents to move discreetly from one part of the complex to another. Children still love to disappear down it and, racing along, appear with cries of delight in unexpected parts of the hill. But only the floor of the palace of the paranoid emperor Domitian retains some of the colour and splendour that once belonged to all the Palatine, and even here the beautiful marble slabs have been so worn and twisted by two millennia of rain and landslide that they resemble a petrified sea.

But in the midst of this desolation, I discovered a spot where I seemed to step back momentarily through a gap in time. It was in the house of Livia, a building that is believed to have been designed for Livia's husband, the emperor Augustus, a giant of a man who in the poet Horace's words, "spread the fame and majesty of our Empire from the sun's bed in the west to the east". His reputation, unlike all the vainglorious monuments I had seen in the Forum, has survived the erosion of time. And so the size of his house came as a shock. It was not much larger than a modern house, and its walls were decorated with murals of fruit and flowers, now softly faded. Here in this modest home, Augustus, "first ruler of the world", had reclined, sipping his watered wine and eating his frugal suppers of bread, cheese and lettuce, while he planned and controlled the lives of the millions for whom the Palatine Hill was the palace of the Monarchy of the Earth, the capital seat of the world. And for a brief moment all ancient Rome—the Rome over whose ruins I had been poring all day—rose up in my mind, as grand and seemingly indestructible as the Vittorio Emanuele Monument of today.

The Moods of the Forum

Against the soaring background of the Palatine Hill, the Roman Forum ruins, of many different periods, now present a single composition of ancient grandeur.

Once the nerve centre of the Republic, then the glittering showpiece of the Empire, the Roman Forum was engulfed by the rising tide of the Dark Ages. Today it is a field of ruins, laid low by time and disturbed anew by industrious archaeologists. In its disordered state it suggests a seashore swept by history's tidal waves; and like a seashore it can show amidst the silted debris unexpected corners of charm and grace—secluded pools where the past lingers in tranquillity. If a wanderer in the Forum chooses to ignore its expanses of featureless brickwork, he is rewarded by a whole succession of separate images, each different from the last and each revealing a mood of the Forum —not as it was when crowded with imperial buildings and the hubbub of a bustling populace, but in the quiet dignity with which the passing centuries have endowed it.

The acanthus plant, which grows wild in the Forum, was once the basis of formalized patterns carved in stone, as on the fallen fragment at right centre.

The Romance of Stone

The growing trees and plants conspire with ancient stones to present an aspect of lonely and melancholy romanticism never contemplated by the ancient Romans, to whom the Forum was a place of crowds and circumstance. It is no wonder that the artists and poets of the 19th Century were inspired by such scenes as dark acanthus leaves framing a shattered marble torso (above) or a tall pillar of veined smoky stone (right) embraced by a shapely tree.

Now enveloped by a tree, this giant column of marble, called cipollino ("onion") because of its markings, once flanked a door to the Temple of Romulus.

The bronze doors to the Temple of Romulus (above) date from the 4th Century. The original lock still works.

Bronze Fifteen Centuries Old

The metal of ancient Rome was bronze; it was freely used to adorn buildings and monuments. But it was so valued by ensuing ages that almost all of it was taken from the Forum for re-use, and thus the Forum today seems a place of brick and stone. Only a few bronze relics, now green and patinated, remain among the stones, as silent reminders of the clang of heavy doors and the clink of coins once heard in this busy centre of Empire.

On the marble floor of the Basilica Emilia, burnt when the Goths sacked Rome in A.D. 410, green stains show where spilt coins were melted by the heat.

Marshalled in a neat row by excavators of the Forum, columns of several different marbles suggest the variety and magnificence of the ancient buildings.

Intimations of Vanished Splendour

Among the dismantled fragments of buildings that lie about in profusion, like the columns and capitals above, a vista will sometimes open out that seems to offer some hint of the extent and splendour of the great temples and basilicas that once stood in the Forum. One of the best preserved places is the House of the Vestal Virgins (right), where honorific statues of some of the Vestals still stand, looking out over their quiet courtyard garden.

A glistening stream of rainwater runs down a path away from one of the Forum's most beautiful attractions—then and now—the House of the Vestal Virgins.

A sight that has stirred the Western imagination in every age is the Roman Forum by moonlight. Here the trees crowning the Palatine Hill are cast into silhouette by the moon's silver light, while in the Forum below the glow of floodlights gilds the fragments of the vanished buildings.

4

The Magnificent Palaces

All morning I had been hunting a will-o'-the-wisp. I was in search of the home of the most infamous of popes—the palace built in about 1460 by Rodrigo Borgia. The Borgias—the Spanish family that set all Rome by the ears during the early 1500s—had always fascinated me. Besides, Rodrigo's home had been almost the first true Renaissance palace in Rome; it marked the end of the chaotic medieval centuries that followed the decline of Imperial Rome and the beginning of a safer and more luxurious age. I thought I knew very nearly where the palace was situated; for while Borgia was still a cardinal his master, Pope Pius II, left a vivid description of it. "All the cardinals who lived along the route had decorated their houses magnificently", Pius wrote, recording the occasion when the head of St. Andrew, rescued from the Saracens, was carried in triumphant procession to St. Peter's. "But all were outstripped in expense and ingenuity by Rodrigo (later Pope Alexander VI). His huge, towering house which he had built on the site of the old mint was covered in rich and wonderful tapestries, He had decorated not only his own house but those near by, so that the square all about them seemed a kind of park full of sweet sounds and songs."

For several hours I wandered along the modern Corso Vittorio Emanuele—the approximate route that the procession had followed, passing south-east from the Vatican into the heart of Rome. But I could not find Borgia's palace. Indeed, I was soon to discover that the houses of the Roman nobility, for all their splendour, blend into the background as though they were shy of attracting attention.

Yet no city in the world is richer in palaces than Rome. There are more than 50 of them crowded into an area a mile in diameter. Some are almost within speaking distance of one another. And it is possible to walk past most of them unawares. The standard Roman building, whether of offices or blocks of flats, contributes to this anonymity because it is designed to classic proportions; the untrained or indifferent eye can pass from an early-20th Century residential block to a late-16th Century palace and note little difference. This camouflage is sometimes abetted by the owner's habit of letting out the ground floor to humdrum trades. So even when you have tracked down a palace, it is possible to be fooled by this disguise, for who ever heard of a prince living above a cobbler's shop?

Yet in many an alley the dirty walls to your right or left may conceal Renaissance interiors furnished at vast expense. Walking through the beetling entrance in a sooty-looking façade, I would find myself in a

Modern diplomatic business has superseded the Renaissance papal intrigues once witnessed by this sumptuous gallery in the 16th-Century Palazzo Farnese. The French embassy now occupies the palace and uses the gallery— whose walls and ceilings are covered by mythological scenes—as a banquet hall.

beautiful courtyard. And if I ventured up the wide stairs and along a corridor or two, I would enter a different world.

But it was rarely as easy as that. Scarcely a palace is open to the public. Most of the old Roman families are still in possession of the buildings their forefathers created, and are too reticent or proud to allow such invasions. To make ends meet, they prefer to let off more and more of the huge buildings, retiring deeper and deeper inside them. It is an eerie business going through the Rome telephone directory and finding these historic family names—names that have been linked with so much splendour and bloodshed—docilely placed in alphabetical order along with insurance agents and bakers. Caetani, Colonna, Doria, Massimo, Orsini—they're all there. You can even telephone them, and although a steward answers the phone, it's a little like telephoning Charlemagne or Joan of Arc.

The Borgias are not in the telephone directory. The Romans had lost no time in obliterating all evidence of the family after its fall from power in the late 16th Century—not so much because of its crimes as because it was openly, boastfully foreign. The Borgias spoke Spanish among themselves, ate Spanish food, even dressed and entertained themselves in the Spanish manner. But the Roman aristocracy, while often replenishing itself from outside, was accustomed to assimilating newcomers until they became more Roman than the Romans. The great families, in fact, were among the most conservative on earth. And they were used to getting their own way not just in Rome but throughout the rest of Italy. When Constantine, the first Christian emperor, moved the seat of empire to Byzantium in A.D. 330, Rome lost much of its reason for existence. Wealth drained from the city and was not replaced. The more able young men took their talents to Constantinople, the new Rome across the sea, and the old Rome began its long dying. Then in the 9th Century occurred that bitter marriage between Italy and Germany that led to the Holy Roman Empire. Shaggy German monarchs rode out of their forests to claim the right to rule the city by virtue of their descent from Charlemagne, the barbarian king who had been crowned Emperor of the West—quite illegally—by the Pope in return for the emperor's protection. Each such claim led to rioting and bloodshed. Yanked back and forth between pope and emperor, Rome fell apart, with the fragments coalescing around a few powerful barons. With no king to suppress them nor, as in other cities, a people vigorous enough permanently to usurp them from below, they grew ever more powerful. And from the ranks of their descendants came the cardinals who elected popes, so creating a closed circle of power.

Of these ancient clans the Colonna claim to be the oldest, tracing their ancestry back to the Etruscan rulers of Tusculum, the deadly enemies of Rome. But probably the family associated the longest with Rome is the Massimo. The story is told how in 1797 Camillo Massimo was asked by Napoleon if it was true that his family descended from the great Roman

The curved outline of the Theatre of Marcellus is still clearly recognizable, in spite of all the changes the structure has undergone since its completion by Augustus in 13 B.C. Fortified in the Middle Ages, it was converted into a palazzo in the 16th Century, and today conceals numerous apartments and even a garden or two.

general Fabius Maximus. With the polite irony of the established addressing the parvenu, Massimo replied: "I could not prove it, the story has only been told in our family for twelve hundred years."

In medieval years, when war between the ancient clans was continual, the home of every noble was a fortified island. Indeed, some of Rome's sturdiest ruins were put to this use by families seeking strongholds for themselves in it: the Orsini moved into the Theatre of Marcellus; the Frangipani took over the Arch of Titus. These fortresses were supplied by provisions of oil, wheat and wine brought in under heavy guard from the family estates in the *Campagna*. The only access between the men's and women's quarters was "the wheel", a kind of one-way revolving door. This was always guarded, less against external enemies than against the ferocious mercenaries with whom each baron strengthened the ranks of his retainers. Even after society became outwardly polite the "wheel" was still in use, and some survive, as a curiosity, today. New palaces—or rather forts—were built to no particular design. But each had its own chapel, its own dungeons (some with access to the Tiber for the disposal of corpses) and its own barracks.

By the end of the 15th Century, although the Throne of St. Peter was still the prize the competing families sought, the papacy had become stable enough to impose order upon the city. But the palaces continued to flourish as corporate institutions because the Roman family is above all

Bees of Prosperity

When in 1623 Cardinal Maffeo Barberini became Pope Urban VIII, the Barberini bees, heraldic sign of his powerful family, began to proliferate in Rome. For Urban VIII was an enthusiastic patron of the arts, and soon the bees were seen like a signature on the magnificent monuments, both public and private, upon which he lavished papal wealth. All the bees illustrated here are details from the decoration of the immense Barberini palace that the Pope began two years after his election, and of its surrounding buildings and gardens. In the coat of arms above the palace's main gate (third from right, middle row) they appear proudly surmounted by the papal tiara and the crossed keys of St. Peter.

patriarchal. Sons, when they married, did not set up house on their own but brought their wives back to the family palace. The first floor was reserved for the head of the family and his wife—hence the term *piano nobile*, or "noble floor", the first floor of all Italian buildings. The eldest son lived on the second floor and the rest of the family fitted in where they could. Servants, retainers, tutors, guards, musicians, scholars under the family patronage—everybody who could claim some relationship or expect material assistance from the family—would be housed in the palace. And over the centuries these palaces grew huge.

It was while I was wandering down the Corso, still unable to find the Borgia's home, that I came to a building that marks the end of one era and the beginning of another. There is no better example of the transition from fort to palace than this: the giant Palazzo di Venezia. Cardinal Pietro Barbo, contemporary and friend of Rodrigo Borgia, began it as early as 1455, and plundered most of its building stone from the Colosseum. By standing on the opposite side of the road it is possible to see, in almost textbook illustration, the gloomy strength of a medieval fortress married to the grace of a Renaissance home. The windows are elegantly arched, and in the courtyard is a handsome loggia; but above them rise battlements and a tower.

I became interested in the Palazzo di Venezia not for its architectural curiosity nor for the museum that now occupies the first floor. I wanted to see the offices of Mussolini. The dictator had taken over the palace in the 1930s, partly for its size and dignity, partly for its central position. But today Mussolini's offices have been forbidden to the general public under the useful label, "Closed for Restoration". When might they be restored and open?, I asked. The attendant shrugged: there was no saying. Could I see the superintendent? The superintendent was, alas, absent. When might she return? Again he shrugged: there was no saying. He sat stolidly behind his barrier of papers and decorative entrance tickets, willing me to go away. The silence lengthened. I found that I was fiddling with a card in my pocket—the visiting card of an important government personage who had urged me to explore the Palazzo di Venezia. It occurred to me that his recommendation might now stand me in good stead. I passed the visiting card over. But before I even had time to say, "He'll vouch for me", the attendant glanced at the name and leapt to his feet. With a startled glance at me, he mumbled an apology and hastened into the office. A few moments passed; a woman, evidently a superior member of the staff, appeared, glanced at me in scarcely veiled surprise and conducted me down endless corridors to a magnificent library. There, again with a murmured apology, she left me. Over the next five minutes or so relays of officials came to the door of the library, peered in at me, looked surprised and then hastened off.

And finally there came the highest official of all, *La Dottoressa* herself, the superintendent of all the museums and galleries of Rome (for the

Photographed in 1931, Mussolini stands behind his office desk in the Palazzo di Venezia. Visitors took nearly a minute to reach him across the enormous room.

Palazzo di Venezia is the headquarters of the *Soprintendenza dei Monumenti*). She looked at me coldly: "You are not Signor ———", she said, referring to the name on the card. "No, of course not. I merely offered the card to establish my bona fides." There was an icy silence while thoughts of the penalties for impersonation whisked through my mind. Then she smiled; then laughed. Her echelons of subordinates smiled and laughed.

"The gentleman may see the offices", she decreed.

It was a long journey. Indeed it might have been planned to illustrate the enormous size of this palace. First there was a quick, claustrophobic descent by lift; then the transit of the museum, dark and gleaming with polish; then a succession of doors, each opened by a different key and each leading into bigger, dustier chambers. Our footsteps echoed; the dust swirled in the light slanting from the windows; we seemed to be receding farther and farther from the everyday world. And at last we gained the vast Sala del Mappamondo. Here, as on a carefully designed stage set, Mussolini used to sit behind his desk while visitors traversed the immense empty space towards him. Into this room had come the ambassadors of the world, jubilant or apprehensive as the war clouds gathered over Europe. As leader of a newborn Italy, Mussolini held—or so it seemed at the time—the balance of power.

There was nothing there now. The room was littered with discarded wine bottles, trestle tables and empty paint tins. I went over to the window that opened on to the famous balcony overlooking the Piazza di Venezia, the balcony from which the dictator played the demagogue with such self-destructive success. The balcony seemed oddly small, scarcely able to hold two people. In the *Sala* there are few reminders either of the man or of his regime. I'd been told that Il Duce had had his portrait depicted in mosaic on the floor; I couldn't find it. The black and white mosaics, worked in the classical style, contain a few bragging slogans: "A new era has begun", "more enemies more honour", and the like; but you have to look hard for Mussolini's portrait. I was reduced at last to asking my guide. Evidently he disapproved of my interest, and at first declined any knowledge of the portrait; then abruptly he strode across the room and ground his heel into a section of the mosaic. "*Ecco Mussolini*". The all-powerful ruler of Italy had chosen to have himself depicted, very small, as a cavorting sea-monster. A sense of humour on his part? An uncharacteristic modesty? Rome is full of surprises.

By now I had strayed far from the possible site of the Borgia's home, for other palaces were luring me away. A stone's throw from the Palazzo di Venezia, where Mussolini lorded it over Rome, I found the Palazzo Doria, where an ancient Roman family defied the dictator. The story of Princess Doria and her wedding ring has now entered the annals of the city. At the time of the Abyssinian War, Mussolini ordered a "voluntary" donation of all wedding rings to augment the country's diminishing stock of gold. In

The fabric of an old city, especially one as cluttered with works of art as Rome, needs continual skilled maintenance. Here a painter redecorates a shrine devoted to the Virgin Mary, taking care not to splatter the ministering angel's wings with paint.

Rome the women trooped up to drop their treasured rings into an urn on the Vittorio Emanuele Monument in the presence of Mussolini himself. Even the Queen of Italy was present and invited the Princess Doria to perform the ceremony with her. The Princess Doria, who was Scottish by birth, declined to do anything of the sort. It was a slap in the face for Mussolini from one of the great families of Rome. Fascist thugs later broke into the Doria palace and caused some damage in revenge, and the name of the near-by street—which for centuries had been the Vicolo Doria—was changed to the Vicolo della Fede (*fede* is the Italian for wedding ring). But Mussolini has gone his way, and the nameplate "Vicolo Doria" can be seen on the wall again.

The means by which the Doria family has survived for centuries in Rome epitomizes the city's own survival by the absorption of new blood. Like the Borgia, the Doria were foreigners; the family originated in Genoa, and the men were great seafarers. Their most famous admiral, Andrea Doria, led the Spanish fleet to victory over the Turks at the Battle of Lepanto in 1571, and brought back as booty some splendid tapestries that are still displayed in the palace. After the family settled in Rome it became, of course, more Roman than the Romans, and acquired the biggest palace of them all— its ground plan is two-thirds the size of St. Peter's. At one time it seemed as if the dynasty would die out; for Andrea Doria had no sons: but he adopted two, and so perpetuated the family name, if not the Doria blood line. Later the Doria formed a marriage alliance with the Pamphili, whose head was Pope Innocent X; and it was with that powerful backing that the family, now known as the Doria-Pamphili, turned its palace into one of the treasure houses of Europe.

The Doria-Pamphili are among the few families that open their homes to the public, but their generosity is tempered by the staff's desire to get it all over and done with. The visitor is left with a whirling indigestion of silk and gold. The elegance of the winter garden, all white marble and drooping ferns; the panelled comfort of the so-called smoking room; Andrea Doria's chamber with the great tapestry of his victory at Lepanto—they are rooms of a lived-in home that yet belongs to history. In the ballroom the music might only just have faded away, and the flowered silk on the walls looks as fresh as the day it was hung. Only in the chapel is there a jarring note—the corpse of St. Theodora in its glass case—but given the Roman preoccupation with death, even this may be thought harmonious. The corpse is dressed in a gay ball dress, now dusty, with tiny glittering gloves drawn over the wizened fingers and a veil pulled mercifully over the head.

The palace's picture gallery leaves the mind reeling. It is a test even for the connoisseur with a guide-book, for the entire collection has, at some stage, been shuffled out of its old order like some enormous pack of cards; and the publisher of the guide-book seems not to have caught up with the changes. Among the welter two faces stand out: Velazquez' portrait of

In a salon of the Palazzo Farnese the French Ambassador and his wife have tea with guests. The palazzo, considered to be Rome's finest, has been the French embassy since 1871. It was begun in 1514 by Sangallo for Alessandro Farnese, later Pope Paul III, and finished in 1589, by della Porta. Michelangelo also worked on it.

Innocent and the marble bust of that Pope's appalling sister-in-law, Donna Olimpia. Velazquez' portrait has been virtually enshrined, for it occupies a little room of its own. Innocent X—most famous of the Pamphili—appears as the epitome of the pope-king, the ruler for whom religion is an incidental. Threatening, implacable, suspicious, he glares out at the observer. Yet this despot before whom all men quailed, himself quailed before another: for Innocent X was ludicrously hag-ridden by Olimpia who dominated him so completely that the Romans called her "*la papessa*". Her portrait bust shows the reasons clearly enough, for the sculptor has frozen, in an instant of time, a most formidable and unpleasant woman.

The story of Innocent's death, and Olimpia's plundering of the papacy, belongs to the realm of moral tales, of cautions against human vanity. It took the old man ten agonized days to die—ten days during which Olimpia prospered. She was reported to have collected a good half-million crowns by selling benefices in the dying man's name. And even that did not satisfy her. Innocent had amassed a treasure—mostly gold coins—in two wooden chests that he kept hidden under his bed. Olimpia nosed them out, and while he was dying she emptied them and made off, leaving the Pope unattended. Others at last had their revenge against the dead tyrant. A servant stole the single brass candlestick that stood by the bed, replacing the candle in a cheap wooden holder. The dead man's relatives refused to pay for his funeral, and Innocent's body, clad in a coarse shirt, was carried to St. Peter's on a bier so short that the feet hung over the edge. A prelate produced five scudi to have the corpse taken away and buried.

But Nemesis waited for Olimpia, too. The next pope ordered her to leave the city and to restore the vast wealth she had stolen. Fortunately for the Doria-Pamphili, the plague took her off before the order could be implemented, and her fortune became part of the family inheritance.

My search for the Borgia palace had by now turned into an exploration of Rome's world of Palazzi. Their number was legion. The Palazzo Barberini, now part of the National Gallery; the Palazzo Borghese, called "the harpsichord" because of its curious shape; the Palazzi Chigi, Quirinal, Corsini, Altemps—the list could continue nearly forever. One morning I wandered through the gardens of the Villa Medici, where Galileo was kept under house arrest for years; the next I burrowed through the apartments of the Palazzo Cancelleria, built by the nephew of a 15th-Century pope with the profits from a single night's gambling. And there were constant surprises. The Palazzo Capranica had been turned into a cinema; the Palazzo dei Penitenzieri into a hotel; and the Palazzo Orsini was built into the fabric of a giant theatre raised by Julius Caesar.

Entry was often unpredictable. The Palazzo Farnese, now the French Embassy, is open for an hour a week on a Sunday morning; but the privilege may be suddenly withdrawn: the first time I tried to gain access, on a wet Sunday in late autumn, I found a crowd of 60 people waiting in the pouring rain at 11 a.m. By 11.30 there was irritation, by midday the beginnings of a riot, led by an enraged Frenchman who informed the impassive, shrugging police that he was being excluded from his national property. At 12.10 the huge door opened a crack and a hand made irritable shooing gestures at the crowd. The Frenchman charged the door and was promptly arrested by the police, presumably threatening an international incident. The hand slammed the door, and the crowd, after calling down curses in half a dozen languages, dispersed.

But when I saw the interior the following week, I realized that the visit had been worthwhile; this is one of the great palaces of the world. Its builder, Cardinal Alessandro Farnese, rose to power through his beautiful sister Giulia, mistress to Pope Alexander VI. "Christ's bride", the wits of Rome called her, and dubbed Alexander "the Petticoat Cardinal". The palace was raised by four successive architects: Antonio da Sangallo (who started it in 1514), Michelangelo, Vignola and della Porta. It is grand, but not forbidding. The stonework is warm and the stairs are generous, so that the visitor finds himself on the first floor, the *piano nobile*, hardly realizing he has ascended 30 feet. There is nothing to break the sweep of the long, beautiful corridors except an occasional statue or tapestry: even the titanic Salon d'Hercule and the riot of mythological figures in the Caracci Gallery are in perfect place.

The Palazzo Farnese is fortunate in its position. In most Roman palaces the visitor becomes afflicted by claustrophobia, the sense of other buildings pressing close, of too-small windows and secret doors. But in front of the

Palazzo Farnese is a wide square, while behind is a beautiful garden that runs down to the Via Giulia.

I must have identified half the palaces of Rome before I at last found the one I sought—the Palazzo Borgia—and then completely by accident. It was midday and I was in the Piazza Sforza-Cesarini on the Corso Vittorio Emanuele. In spite of the burning sun, the little square was cool and green —it was almost like being underwater—for chestnut trees rose out of its gravel and interlocked their branches 15 feet overhead. The piazza has a quiet life of its own. The secondhand bookseller, with his racks of engravings, places himself on the Corso side of the square like a fisherman extending his net against the current. Those who buy his wares drift to a halt under the trees, and sometimes relax in one of the restaurants that surround the piazza, Hot, tired, I sank on to a restaurant seat, ordered a long drink and indulged in a very Roman pastime: that of watching the world go by. When at length I asked for my bill, I looked casually at its heading—and there, beneath the name of the café, I read the words: "The home of Lucrezia Borgia".

And so it proved. The restaurant was probably the birthplace of Rodrigo Borgia's notorious children—Lucrezia and Cesare—for their mother had a house here next to her lover's palace. The palace itself, with its narrow windows, thick walls and embrasures for cannon, stood close by—almost the first true Renaissance palace in Rome, for its interior was gaily furnished and decorated. And the square in which I now sat was the same square that Pope Pius II had described 500 years earlier as being a "park full of sweet sounds and songs".

Such experiences are typical of Rome. The palaces alone hold a thousand such associations. But it is as living works of art, rather than as historical museums, that they are most memorable. Their great families had at their service some of the finest architects and painters the world has known, and they made good use of them. For whatever reasons—a hunger for prestige or a vulgar love of display—they raised a remarkable heritage. Now, with their descendants withdrawing farther and farther inside these magnificent husks, the improvidence of the Farnese clan and the pomp of the Barberini have gone forever. But the vision of the architect remains, and Rome is still the richer for it.

Il Duce's Grandiose Heritage

Along its die-straight course, E.U.R.'s main thoroughfare, Via Cristoforo Colombo, intersects two vast plazas surrounded by grandiose buildings of the 1930s.

Dictator Benito Mussolini undertook to build a "Third Rome" that would rival in grandeur the Romes of Imperial and Renaissance times. His most ambitious project was E.U.R. (above in a panoramic aerial view), named for an exposition— *Esposizione Universale di Roma*—which was to have opened in 1942 to commemorate 20 years of Fascist rule. The exhibition never took place; but E.U.R. survives as a smart suburb, its

streets and buildings as rigidly ordered as the political movement they were designed to celebrate. It has been called Rome's greatest town-planning achievement since the time of the emperor Trajan and, with less enthusiasm, the "least offensive" of Il Duce's efforts. Although he failed to achieve his aim of Rome's "triumphal return to its highest traditions", Mussolini managed one thing—for better or worse he left his mark on the city.

The motifs of Mussolini's Rome glorified Fascism and, chiefly, Mussolini.

Paint blotches show that feelings still run high about the Fascist era.

In Praise of Self

Mussolini tried to claim an Imperial inheritance with forms taken from antiquity. Mosaics like ancient Roman floors appear at the Foro Italico, in north-west Rome, a sports centre named for the Forum of old. Arches of the Palazzo della Civiltà del Lavoro— Palace of the Workers (right)—so clearly evoke Rome's best-known building that it is nicknamed "the square colosseum".

The Palazzo della Civiltà del Lavoro extols Italians from poets to settlers overseas in a bold inscription and other heroes and heroines in rows of statuary.

The Museo della Civiltà Romana, a popular museum devoted to the history and character of Roman civilization, features thick columns rising to an open roof.

Fascist realism meant heroic nudity for a skier.

A discus thrower's muscled arm is held up by a bar.

Casual drapery constitutes a tennis player's attire.

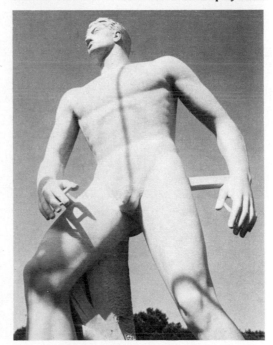

Even the fingers of this monolith require bracing.

The Overblown Monuments of Fascism

In scale as well as form, Mussolini's designers sought to imitate their Imperial forebears. At times the result was an architectural evocation of power, as in the bulky columns of the Museo della Civiltà Romana (left). In other instances, such as the twice-life-sized statues representing physical fitness in the Foro Italico (above), the sculptors' attempts to achieve awesome massiveness instead achieve a phoney grandeur reminiscent of Il Duce himself.

The Palazzo dei Congressi, with its broad and handsome mosaic terrace, is used for large conferences.

A Forceful Geometry

Many of the changes wrought by Il Duce on Rome have been harshly criticized. His planners ruthlessly drove roads through some areas of historical importance and it is doubtful whether public taste will ever embrace all of his architectural contributions as structures of beauty. But a few works, such as the fan-patterned pavement above and the church at right, both to be found in E.U.R., are esteemed by some modern architects.

The stark lines and the impressive bulk of E.U.R.'s Church of Ss. Peter and Paul achieve a striking effect. Its dome is nearly as large as that of St. Peter's.

5

The Bishop of Rome

By about 11.30 on a Sunday morning the huge square embraced by the arms of Bernini's colonnade in front of St. Peter's is beginning to fill. There is a casual, family atmosphere about the crowd. Romans pay attention to their clothes, but those in the square seem even neater than usual, with their little girls in a froth of frills and bows. On a hot Sunday the jets of the giant fountains soar in the air with a gratifying coolness, and clusters of people stand around them.

By midday the crowd has grown to the size of a small army—and still there is room for more. On the stroke of noon a gun booms from the near-by Janiculum Hill; the birds rise, and there is an outburst of handclapping as a tiny figure in white appears high up at one of the windows of the Vatican Palace. His appearance gives a human proportion by which to measure the surrounding buildings, and one becomes aware of the gigantic scale upon which St. Peter's and the Vatican are built. The handclapping is welcoming rather than ecstatic; similarly, the old man's voice that sounds over the speakers is friendly and relaxed—talking, not sermonizing. At the end of the soliloquy his distant hand moves in the graceful gesture of benediction; throughout the crowd there is a flutter of hands in response. On St. Peter's a bell begins to beat in a bass so deep that it sounds as a continuous growl, and the week's Angelus blessing is at an end.

The fact that the Vicar of Christ, the Supreme Pontiff and Universal Pope, The Servant of the Servants of God, is also Rome's bishop has at once caused many of the city's tragedies and triumphs. For nearly two thousand years—more than two-thirds of Rome's existence—the city's ruler has been a priest-king—the most archaic of all sovereign powers, a type born in pre-history and surviving into the era of nation states. The Vatican is a fact of political life and we accept it with familiarity, but its survival is truly extraordinary. If the Pharaohs were still wielding power by the Suez Canal or the Aztecs in Mexico City, it would be scarcely less remarkable than that the successor of the Apostle Peter still holds absolute power over a tiny but precisely delineated section of a modern metropolis.

As temporal ruler, the Pope is monarch of the Vatican City State, an enclave of only 108 acres—1/140th the size of San Marino, the oldest and smallest independent republic in the world. The Vatican has 30 streets and squares, 50 palaces, eight grand staircases, 200 smaller ones, anywhere from 10,000 to 11,000 rooms (even the architects cannot keep an accurate count because of the partitioning and repartitioning of space that is forever going on), two churches in addition to St. Peter's, and

The door beneath the draped-marble glory of Bernini's tomb of Pope Alexander VII in St. Peter's is normally shut. When it is opened, visitors get a back-corridor glimpse framed by the masterpiece, a graphic illustration of the contrast between the Vatican's museum-like face and the busy working world beyond it.

innumerable chapels, including the two most famous, the Sistine and Pauline Chapels, in which Michelangelo's great frescos may be seen. The Vatican also has two jails (only one is used today), a radio station, a railway station, an underground garage, a printshop (which has printed the Lord's Prayer in 250 languages), a cobbler's shop, a pharmacy, a clinic, a supermarket and, in the warrens of St. Peter's, even a small bar. Like any other independent state, it has its own flag—a yellow and white one, with emblems of staff, tiara and crossed keys.

The most important occupant of this city is the Vicar of Christ, responsible for the spiritual well-being of 600 million Catholics. The Pope exercises his authority over the Church through a recently streamlined bureaucracy. Foremost of the papal advisory bodies is the College of Cardinals. The day-to-day activities of the Church are left to the Roman Curia, or Holy See, with its various departments presided over by cardinals, archbishops and bishops. The Pope himself has to be an able administrator. There is a story told that Pope Paul, in his long climb through the bureaucracy of the Church to the papacy, came to know its workings so well that when his new Secretary of State could not find a certain paper the pontiff wanted, Paul said, "Filing cabinet 17 in the third room, second drawer, fifth folder back."

In spite of its complexity the Vatican is a smooth-running organization. The last public assessment of its efficiency was undertaken independently by the American Institute of Management in 1956 as part of a study of the Church's central and local administration. The object was to see how well or how poorly the Vatican functioned. The Vatican came out with flying colours. Out of a possible 10,000 points, the Institute gave it 8,800.

How did all this come to be? How did such power coalesce around the Pope in Rome? The Roman Catholics look to the New Testament for the answer. The Vatican's authority rests on the argument that Christ founded a new society, namely the Church, and provided a government for the Church by conferring governmental powers on his disciple Peter who passed them on—thus ensuring the continuation of the Church. ("And I say also to thee, that thou art Peter, and upon this rock I will build my Church; and the gates of hell shall not prevail against it. And I will give unto thee the keys of the Kingdom of Heaven: and whatsoever thou shalt bind on earth shall be bound in heaven: and whatsoever thou shalt loose on earth shall be loosed in heaven.")

A Christian community existed in Rome in A.D. 50, when Peter is believed to have come to the city for the first time. With Peter's crucifixion a dozen or so years later in the Circus of Nero, the papal succession began. By the end of the 1st Century, Christianity had spread throughout the Empire, and by the close of the 2nd Century, Christianity, Catholicism and Roman primacy had become synonomous terms, with the pope the supreme pontiff, the bishop of bishops, the bishop of Rome. It remained for a 5th Century pope, Leo I, to formulate the doctrine of succession. He based it

The physical "plant" of the Vatican, which includes structures up to 1,500 years old, requires constant maintenance. Much of it is done by Sanpietrini—skilled climbers like the one here dangling from a rope just to pull weeds from a wall of St. Peter's. Most of the Sanpietrini—literally St. Peterites—inherit their jobs from their fathers.

on the Roman law of inheritance by which the heir inherits the deceased's assets and liabilities but not, of course, his personal qualifications, distinctions and merits. The doctrine distinguished between the person of the Pope and the Office. What mattered for purposes of government and papal succession was the Office: a pope could be a saint, a mediocrity or a rogue, but the papacy and the Church would survive.

During subsequent centuries, by a mixture of force and skill, the papacy gained control over a huge section of Italy—17,200 square miles in all—that stretched from Rome almost to Venice. The rule of the popes over these States of the Church was no worse, if not detectably better, than that of the other Italian princes in their areas. But in order to maintain political power in an embattled society, the papacy found that it had to enter the arena on the same terms as the princes. And there were plenty of Italians to protest at this degradation of a sacred charge, and to lament the endless power-seeking. "It is now more than a thousand years since these territories and cities have been given to the priests", complained Giovanni de' Mussi, the chronicler of Piacenza, about 1350, "and ever since then the most violent wars have been waged on their account, and yet the priests neither now possess them in peace, nor will ever be able to possess them. It were in truth better before the eyes of God and the world that these pastors should entirely renounce the temporal dominium. How is it possible that there has never been any good pope to remedy such evils and that so many wars have been waged for these transient possessions? Truly we cannot serve God and Mammon at the same time, cannot stand with one foot in Heaven and the other on Earth."

The passionate sincerity of de' Mussi's cry sounds even through his crabbed Latin, and over the following centuries the quotation was to become virtually the anthem not only for anti-papists but of all those who wanted Italy again to become one nation. So entrenched was the papacy in the heart of Italy, and so entangled in the complexities of politics, that a surgical operation was needed to remove it. This operation was performed on the morning of 20th September, 1870—in a dramatic event that was the culmination of years of revolutionary work. That morning news came to the mild-mannered but adamantine Pope Pius IX that the armed forces of the new King of Italy had forced a breach in the ancient city walls by the Porta Pia, and that the papal troops were falling back. Pius IX ordered that the white flag of surrender be hoisted over the papacy's fortress, Castel Sant'Angelo, and so brought to an end the Pope's temporal dominion over all territories in Italy, except for the Vatican City itself. Pius retired into his palace, and to demonstrate that he was bowing to superior force and not to law, he refused to leave the sanctity of the Vatican for the crass world of the politicized Rome outside. He refused even to give that fatherly blessing to the crowds in St. Peter's Square—and so was born the legend of the Prisoner of the Vatican.

At an ordination ceremony in St. Peter's Square the scene is recorded by a soberly dressed photographer from one of the two official papal photographic firms. The Felici family business, now in its fourth generation, has been receiving papal commissions for over a hundred years, and the firm of Giordani, still run by its original founder, for about 50 years.

His three successors followed his lead until, in 1929, Pius XI and Benito Mussolini agreed to the Lateran Pacts. By these treaties, the Holy See recognized the existence of the kingdom of Italy, while the Italian government, as well as bestowing great financial and legal benefits on the Vatican, recognized the Pope's sovereignty over the Vatican. Mussolini—with the approval of Pope and Curia—then perpetrated an architectural atrocity: through the rich tangle of streets between the Tiber and St. Peter's Square he drove the arid, arrow-straight Via della Conciliazione.

The Vatican City, *Città del Vaticano*, is a parvenu among Roman institutions. A few of its buildings appeared as early as the 6th Century, but until 1377—during most of the existence of the Roman Catholic Church—the official home of the Pope was elsewhere. On the other side of the city was the Palace of St. John Lateran. This great church was known as the "Mother and Head of the Churches in the City and the World". It was the first basilica built in Rome and the first place where Christians could worship in freedom outside the catacombs. St. John Lateran contained some of the most sacred Christian relics, including the reputed heads of the apostles Peter and Paul. Built into the palace was the Scala Santa—the marble steps that were said to have come from Pilate's judgement-hall in Jerusalem, where Christ Himself had trodden. In medieval times the Lateran Palace grew enormous; but it was burnt down in the 14th Century in one of the innumerable riots of those times. And instead of rebuilding it, the popes moved their seat to the Vatican Hill.

The hill lay on the opposite side of the Tiber from Rome, outside the walls of Rome. Up to Nero's day its lower levels were no more than a fetid marsh, while the sparsely-populated higher levels produced nothing but a thin, harsh wine. But as the population of Rome expanded, even this area acquired value. Part of it became a cemetery, and over a portion of it Nero built his huge circus. It was in this circus, about A.D. 64, that the Apostle Peter was said to have been crucified. The same strong but undocumented tradition claims that Peter was buried in the near-by cemetery and that a modest memorial was raised above the grave.

When the emperor Constantine wanted to build the first great Christian church, he naturally chose this site, erecting the basilica of St. Peter over the tomb. According to legend, Constantine carried away the first 12 baskets of rubble with his own hands, then an army of workmen descended on the site. Theirs was a formidable task. The basilica was to be enormous, as big as anything that had been built in the pagan world. To erect it on the sloping site, a huge platform had to be created; in the process the cemetery was smothered with clay and rubble. Thus sealed, it remained untouched for centuries, providing a priceless archaeological record when the search for Peter's grave began in the mid-20th Century.

The builders of the basilica also cannibalized other monuments, starting a practice that was to prove more destructive to Rome than the raids of

Like the switchboards in administrative centres of other multinational organizations, this one in the Vatican deals routinely with calls from all parts of the world. Besides the lack of usual switchboard paraphernalia, its obvious distinguishing characteristic is the dress of its operators. Nuns handle the bulk of the Vatican's massive clerical workload.

barbarians. The near-by Circus of Nero was an obvious source of building material, but far more beautiful structures were plundered too, such as the Pantheon and the remains of the Forum. The basilica of St. Peter's seems to have been raised in haste—the great columns for its interior were brought from several temples and erected confusedly; in some cases the architects did not even give a column its correct base and capital. But although the basilica must have seemed ugly to conservative Romans, used to purer architecture, it symbolized the triumph of Christianity over the paganism of ancient Rome. Yet in spite of its swift construction, the church was to dominate Rome for over 1,200 years. Only in the mid-15th Century did the dismantling of the old church begin, a job that would take nearly a century to complete, and not until 1626 would the present St. Peter's, which took another century to build, stand in its place.

For 50 years after its foundation the old basilica remained unscathed. The enemies of Rome were mostly fellow-Christians, and however bitter the hatred between sect and sect, they all revered those few square feet of earth—the tomb of Peter—that lay deep beneath the building. But in 846, Muslim raiders, inspired by religious hatred and a desire for plunder, stripped the basilica even of the silver plating on its doors.

The citizens of Rome proper were safe enough across the river, but they could only watch helplessly while the basilica of St. Peter's on the other side was sacked. And the invaders, taking most of their loot with them, escaped in their ships down the Tiber. The reigning Pope Leo IV swore that

never again would the tomb of Peter be so defiled. Under his direction the entire Vatican area was walled in. The work was completed in 852. A circumvallation over 40 feet high—with 48 towers and three gates—swept up from the Tiber to the crest of the Vatican Hill and down again to join the river downstream. Thus the Vatican became a walled town; it was named, after Leo, the *Civitas Leonina*, the Leonine City.

But the chief defence of the Leonine City was an enormous cylindrical mass of a building which had been constructed before the walls were built. It was known as Castel Sant'Angelo, and it had been raised by the emperor Hadrian as his family mausoleum. This imposing structure was in the form of a giant drum, whose top was covered by earth and planted with cypresses. From its centre rose a tower surmounted by a statue, possibly of the sun god. A spiral passageway wound through the core of the cylinder to the sepulchral chamber. The whole building, enormously solid, might have been custom-designed as a fortress. One hundred and thirty years after it had been finished, the emperor Aurelian was the first to recognize its military potential; he transformed it into a bastion. By the 5th Century it had become an important part of Rome's defences, and it had been embellished with six towers, windows for archers and battlements for catapults.

During the plague of 590, Pope Gregory saw on top of the fortress an angel sheathing his sword—which was interpreted as a sign that the plague had ended. In gratitude, a marble statue of an angel was substituted for Hadrian's sun god, and from that time on the fortress-tomb became

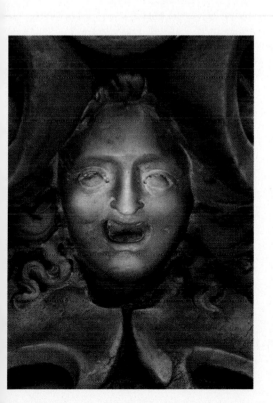

Birth of a Baby

Amid the splendour of St. Peter's wealth of sacred art, the poignant sculptures seen here, decidedly human in scale and subject matter, are often overlooked by visitors. They are carved on the marble pedestals that support the four spiral columns of the *baldacchino*, Bernini's great bronze canopy above the papal altar (page 128); they show a woman's face contorted by pain of mounting intensity (left) and, on the last pedestal, the head of a smiling baby (right).

Legend says that Pope Urban VIII commissioned Bernini to create the *baldacchino* and its narrative in stone in thanksgiving after his favourite niece had survived a difficult childbirth. If so, an uncle's concern and the expression of his gratitude provided one of the first realistic portrayals of labour, and conferred artistic celebrity to an otherwise forgotten 17th-Century child.

known as Castel Sant'Angelo—The Castle of the Holy Angel. In 1753 a bronze angel replaced the marble one; and it remains in place today.

Over the centuries successive popes added ceremonial and living quarters to the bastion, creating a little refuge in the sky for themselves. To me Castel Sant'Angelo is one of the most satisfying of all Rome's ancient monuments. It is also one of the best cared for. In the entrance porch there are five models showing the stages of the building's metamorphosis from tomb to fortress.

Castel Sant'Angelo typifies the paradoxes of Rome—in this case in the contrasting sections of the structure. All fortress-prisons have macabre histories, and Castel Sant'Angelo's may be the most bloodstained of all. For nearly 1,500 years it was witness to countless human agonies: no horror that man can perpetrate was neglected within its walls. Here John X was smothered, Benedict VI was strangled and John XIV died of starvation or poison. But while an aura of evil haunts the terrible dungeons, the upper area is a gay, friendly place to spend a morning. This is due in part to its elevation above the city and in part to the fact that its buildings are cool and their decorations delightful; the whole place breathes an atmosphere of relaxation.

The promenade at the top of the castle became one of my favourite calling points in the city, well worth the long ascent. There is an extra-ordinary sensation of unfolding history as you move around here. If you walk slowly and look outwards the impression is conveyed that the whole top of the building is turning, as vista after vista of the city comes into sight.

Connecting the castle to the Vatican via part of the wall that encloses the Vatican is a high, covered walk by which the inhabitants of the palace could reach the castle during times of danger. Clement VII used it during the sack of Rome in 1527; the historian Paolo Govio records how he threw his purple monsignor's cloak over Clement's white habit to make him less conspicuous to the rioting soldiers below.

Today most visitors to the Vatican approach it from the Via della Conciliazone, Mussolini's sterile street running up from the Tiber. Along the route lies the *Banca di Sancto Spirito*—the Bank of the Holy Spirit—which many people assume is Vatican property. It is not, and never has been (although the Vatican does hold an 8 per cent interest in it). Ahead looms the dome of St. Peter's. It can be seen from almost anywhere in Rome, and now as one approaches, it seems to tip backwards and partially disappear behind the massive façade of the church.

The interior of St. Peter's is so huge, the proportions so grand that the individual is reduced almost to insignificance in the scale of things. Hour after hour, day after day, year after year, groups of awed strangers drift across the marble floors of the church, heads craned, eyes dazzled. There is an endless murmur of guides rattling off statistics, anecdotes, explanations. Kneeling oblivious among the crowds are people praying. Here and

Near these 1st-Century funereal niches beneath the basilica that bears his name, excavators during the 1940s uncovered what is thought to be the grave of St. Peter. The bones were those of a large-framed man who fitted descriptions of the Apostle; among the bones were remnants of purple cloth embroidered with gold.

there, dwarfed by the immensity of the magnificent structure are plain wooden confessionals, with a notice attached to each indicating what language the priest within speaks.

If you enter St. Peter's before midday, preferably early in the morning you will see another deeply moving, yet routine event: solitary priests, each attended by a single acolyte, hurrying across the marble pavement to one of the innumerable side chapels. The acolytes are Romans, slightly bored and sometimes mischievous boys. The priests are foreigners each utterly absorbed in what is one of the great moments of his life: the opportunity to say Mass in St. Peter's, the mother church. Every priest in every country of the world has the right to say Mass here at least once in his life. And all who come to Rome exercise the right, even though it means that they must book a chapel months in advance.

St. Peter's remains the great magnet, the Pope the great spiritual figure to whom the faithful are drawn. It is significant that although many Romans are anti-clerical, they are intensely loyal to their bishop. Even the most strident Communist propaganda carefully distinguishes between the Pope and the Vatican, and avoids attacking either the person or the Office of the supreme pontiff. Within the Vatican itself I became aware of this very Latin approach to the Pope. What was it like, I asked, when one's boss—the equivalent of the chairman or managing director of a company—was also the representative of Christ on earth, the infallible leader of the world's Roman Catholics? None of the officials to whom I spoke had any difficulty answering the question honestly. Nothing unusual about it at all, they said. I found, indeed, an engaging lack of stuffiness among Vatican officials in their attitude towards The Boss. They were perfectly prepared to discuss his ordinary human shortcomings. But they also showed a deep and natural piety towards The Boss in his God-given role.

To a degree the Pope must find himself a victim of his high office and Vatican bureaucracy. Still, each pope has managed to project his own personality. The austere Pius XII seemed to keep the world at arm's length; John XXIII delighted in being part of the world; Paul VI ventured out into it when he took his precedent-breaking journeys to the United States, the Middle East and India to demonstrate and proclaim that the Bishop of Rome was also the Universal Pope, the universal father.

For long it was argued that only an Italian could be a pope—only an Italian could thread his way through the maze of what was basically an Italian bureaucracy. But now that the bureaucracy has been modernized, this no longer has quite the same validity. The last non-Italian pope was the Dutchman Adrian VI. Perhaps another non-Italian will follow in his steps one day. But practical considerations must be taken into account, and one of these is politics. A pope from one of the major powers might be suspected of too much allegiance to his own country, whereas Italian popes have proved they can serve without a national prejudice.

One of the Vatican's most modern features is the audience hall designed by Pier Luigi Nervi and built in 1971. Some 7,500 people a week seek papal audiences like this one. During the last Holy Year the hall's 8,000 seats were not enough; requests rose to 35,000 a week, and most audiences took place in St. Peter's Square.

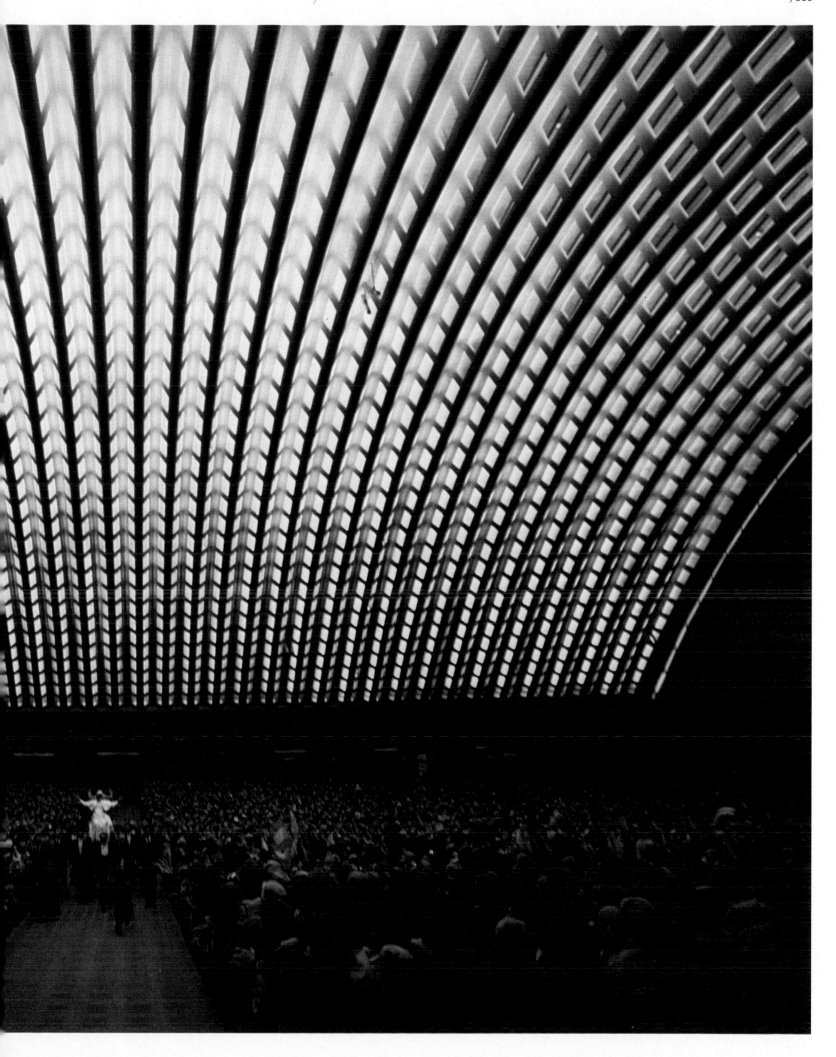

However busy he may be, the Pope must seem at all times accessible. In addition to the weekly ceremony in St. Peter's Square he holds regular audiences that anyone—Muslim or Hindu, as well as Catholic—can attend. All that is necessary is to obtain a pass from an embassy. The audience can take place in St. Peter's itself, in the square outside when the weather is warm, or even in the Vatican's most strikingly modern structure, the hall built by Pier Luigi Nervi in 1971. An outdoor audience may draw 30,000 to 40,000 ticket holders, with another 10,000 to 20,000 able to see the goings-on from behind the fences erected to contain the invited. For such an occasion the Pope is not carried on his regal chair, but is driven from the Gate of Bells into the square, standing in a Jeep. His route takes him past the obelisk in the square so that he traverses the crowd in a half-circle.

Nervi's hall seats 8,000 and has standing room for another 4,000; when some of the chairs are removed, 14,000 people can use the chamber. In spite of the large crowds and the newness of the architecture, the atmosphere is still reverential, although infused by a tincture of the cinema. The hall is handsomely proportioned, the ceiling a single curve whose parallel rows of herring-bone lights give a curious rippling effect. An organ and two stained-glass windows contribute an ecclesiastical note. But the stage is inescapably theatrical and looks rather like the setting for an historical play. As backcloth there is one of the priceless Raphael tapestries from the Vatican galleries. In front is the papal throne. Four Swiss Guards, complete with helmets, plumes and halberds, stand sentinel behind. The Guards are everywhere, some in the finery that Michelangelo is said to have designed for them, some in the sober eggplant colour of their working dress.

From time to time one or another of the national groups in the auditorium starts to sing a hymn in its own language, and the organ picks up the theme. In spite of the long wait—an hour or more—there is no impatience. For most of the people this is the culmination of months, even years, of saving and planning. They are probably here for the first and last time in their lives, and are content to gaze and record. But at length there is a stir, and the papal party enters, the Pope carried high above the crowd on his portable throne. A burst of handclapping gives the feel of a thunderstorm, while hundreds of camera bulbs flash like lightning. Brought to the stage, the Pope welcomes each group in its own language. After the fervour of anticipation, the actual audience is friendly and informal. But the moment of blessing at the end is highly charged, as if something was actually passing from the small, remote figure on the stage to the massed thousands before him.

Because the Pope must appear open to all, his security is one of the Vatican's chief problems. In addition to the normal security surrounding a head of state is that needed to keep religious fanatics at bay. For each of the hundreds of millions of Roman Catholics in the world, the Bishop of Rome is the focus of his faith. And some of those millions assume that they have the right of continuous access to him. There are also the homicidal lunatics who would regard the assassination of the head of the Roman Catholic Church as a religious act. So the Vatican security forces try to keep track of all visitors all the time. Everyone is issued a pass upon which his destination is stated. Should he stray off the route, attracted by some beguiling aspect of the gardens, a guard will appear from nowhere, uttering that universal Roman query—"*Dica!*" and check the destination noted on the visitor's card. These guards—mainly members of the Vatican's new security force, *Servizio di Vigilanza* wear civilian blue suits and carry sidearms. Trained by the Italian state, they are in constant contact with Italian Intelligence and police officials, who warn them when there is the slightest possibility of danger. Walking alongside and behind the Pope during ceremonies, they scan the crowds constantly.

The security force that most people notice on a visit to the Vatican, however, are not these but the colourful Swiss Guards. They form the pontiff's personal bodyguard, and also furnish the sentries for palace entranceways. In spite of their decorative appearance, they perform much more than a decorative function. I once spent half an hour with a Lieutenant of the Guard at the great Bronze Gate, the ceremonial entrance into the palace proper. The gate opens into an immense gallery, at the far end of which rises Bernini's regal staircase, the Scala Regia. In the shadows at the foot of these steps is another sentry. his wasp-striped uniform of orange, blue and red half-dissolving into the gloom.

The lieutenant I interviewed was a powerfully-built man named Hans Roggen. He had established himself at a battered wooden table just inside the gate, incongruous in the marble splendour. Two motionless sentries with halberds stood at the entrance. Every five minutes or so, while I was talking with Lieutenant Roggen, a tourist would come up to the gate and look inside. Roggen would continue talking to me, but the moment a person stepped over the threshold, he would cover the 50 feet to the gate with the explosive speed of a samurai and courteously but implacably turn the intruder away. During the height of the tourist season he would be turning away people of all nationalities for eight hours a day, day after day, and each would be treated with the same courtesy.

A further precaution is generally not known: a square box, two and a half feet high and slightly tapered towards the top, hidden at one side of the Bronze Gate. Inside are three sub-machine guns, fully loaded, ready for action—and the Swiss Guards are highly trained professional soldiers who know how to use them. Roggen himself keeps at his side a small attaché case that contains one service automatic and one can of anti-riot gas.

The Swiss Guard was formed by the warrior-pope Julius II in the 16th Century. The Guard's total loyalty—literally to the death—has earned it its favoured place close to the pontiff. The two guards who stand outside the entrance to the papal study have orders to let no one in except the

The ornate 16th-Century uniforms of the Vatican's Swiss Guard are deceptive. The Guard is not a purely ceremonial unit but a highly trained security force of professional soldiers who serve as the Pope's personal bodyguard. Except when on show, as they are in this inspection by a prelate, they are usually armed with rifles rather than halberds.

Pope's secretaries, the Prefect of the Apostolic Palace and those the Prefect authorizes. They also refuse to accept any messages for delivery to the Pope except those from cardinals, delivered by the cardinals themselves. Cardinals are the only people in the Church privileged to make their thoughts known to the Pope at any time in writing. They hand the guards their envelopes inscribed, "For the Sacred Table of the Holy Father", and they may be sure these will be opened by no one save the Pope himself.

The total number of the Guard is about a hundred, although this can vary. Recruits are drawn exclusively from the ranks of Swiss conscripts: about the time that a likely citizen soldier in Switzerland is nearing the end of his service he is approached on behalf of the Guard. If he accepts, he signs on for a minimum period of three years, at a good basic pay and with the right to marry if he wishes. During the swearing-in ceremony in one of the Vatican's courtyards, each guard takes the oath of allegiance in his own tongue—German, French, or Italian, depending upon the part of Switzerland he comes from. He grips the Swiss Guard banner with his left hand and raises two fingers and the thumb of his right to symbolize the Trinity.

A guard's life tends to be a good one, and he lives well ("Too well", Roggen said ruefully, looking down at his generous proportions). The fact that many sign on again after their first term—Roggen was at the end of his eighth year—argues that they appreciate their unusual role. When they end their engagement, most return home—and perhaps inspire the next generation to carry a halberd for the Bishop of Rome.

The Guards are among the relatively few people to live within the Vatican. The resident population is thought to number less than a thousand. Even some of the cardinals and prelates reside outside. The total workforce numbers about 3,500. Through the secondary gate of St. Anna, at approximately 8 a.m., pass the Vatican employees who live outside the walls on their way to their various jobs. The guards know every face, and any newcomer is immediately halted.

These workers perform a range of services, from stocking and running a cafeteria to manning the radio station. Some work in the post office, some for the rather staid daily newspaper, *Osservatore Romano*, which has a circulation of 90,000. The Vatican radio broadcasts in 33 languages and puts out approximately a hundred programmes a day. The post office has become increasingly popular with Roman citizens because it is far more efficient than that of the Italian government.

Uncertainty pervades many of the Vatican's facts and figures. In public relations the authorities tend to be paradoxical. On the one hand, the Vatican generously makes its treasures available to the public; the galleries are the best administered in Rome, and the exhibits are beautifully displayed. On the other hand, there is a great reticence even about inoffensive facts—such as the population figure. Information is available but widely scattered, and the curious are thrown back on the gaudy little

Among the treasures in the Vatican archives is King Henry VIII's unsuccessful petition for a Church-sanctioned divorce from Catherine of Aragon, bearing the wax seals of all those who signed it. When it was denied, Henry—and England—turned Protestant.

booklets, mostly written in a sycophantic style, that pass as popular guides.

Vatican finances are the most closely guarded secret in the enclave, known only to a few. About the only sum known with any certainty is the £17 million ($83 million) that was paid to Pope Pius XI after the signing of the Concordat with the Fascist government. The Pope has a special administration to handle the Vatican's investments. These have been put at between £125 million ($250 million) and £250 million ($500 million), but such an estimate does not include donations from parishes the world over, nor such Vatican properties as churches and works of art like Michelangelo's "Pietà" in St. Peter's, so priceless that no value can be placed on it—and no earnings come from it since it is there for all to see without charge. Out of its income the Vatican must pay for the maintenance of the City State itself, provide support for dioceses too poor to be self-supporting and pay the expenses of those who come to Rome from impoverished areas on church business.

"You can't blame them", a Vatican prelate responded when I mentioned official reticence concerning finances and other matters. "Every word they utter is picked up and weighed and—as like as not—distorted." He gave a personal example. Some years ago, when Pope Paul VI was breaking precedent by his series of global journeys, the prelate wrote an article speculating on the possibilities of a papal visit to Great Britain. The prelate is a Scotsman, with a wry sense of humour. Tongue in cheek, he pointed out that the only part of the British Isles where a pope could tactfully land was Scotland; a Vatican Bull had deposed King John in 1211 and England, unlike Scotland, was therefore still legally under the jurisdiction of the papacy. Thus the Pope's visit might be an embarrassing reminder. It was the kind of elaborate joke beloved of ecclesiastical scholars, and it would have circulated only among fellow prelates chuckling over the part as they read their scholarly journals. An enterprising American journalist noticed it, however, and requested permission to reproduce it in his newspaper. The prelate assented—and later saw his scholarly sally presented to the lay readership under the banner headline: "Elizabeth II A Squatter, Vatican Documents Prove".

This Scottish cleric has worked in the Secret Archives of the Vatican for the past 17 years. He has become amiably resigned to the fact that his duties will be regularly interrupted by scholars hoping to be shown round. The term Secret Archives seems to be yet further proof of the Vatican desire to keep itself to itself, never to explain, never to apologize. But my informant points out that the word "secret" here comes merely from the Latin root of the word for "secretary"; the archives, in fact, are open to any *bona fide* scholar, providing the documents that he is searching for are at least one hundred years old. (Newer documents are indeed kept under lock and key.)

The archivists have evolved a kind of guided tour through their treasures, and to pace down these book-lined alleyways, pausing now and then to glance at some outstanding treasure, is to become aware again of the awesome weight of the centuries in Rome. At the end of the tour the visitor is brought to a modern vault in which are preserved documents that even the Vatican considers unusually valuable. With a touch of proprietorship—like somebody showing off the family heirlooms— the prelate brings out some of the more fascinating: an impatient demand for payment from Michelangelo; the last letter from Mary Queen of Scots; a handsomely bound missive of St. Teresa of Avila, presented by General de Gaulle to the Pope; a letter from the nephew of Genghis Khan, politely declining to become a Christian; Henry VIII's application for divorce with its mass of seals; all these lie side by side in their narrow trays.

The parts of the Vatican that are accessible to the public should be sufficient to occupy most curious people for a lifetime. As with the Forum, the only way to come to terms with the profusion of treasures is to return again and again, leaving as soon as mental indigestion starts. The galleries adopt the inhospitable Roman habit of not labelling exhibits, and a guide —either printed or human—is essential. Every day the galleries are open they are packed. The corridor level descends slightly, and standing near the entrance you can look over the massed heads and see people perhaps half a mile away in marble halls. The impression is of some vast, organic whole flowing like a sea through the passageways.

Everybody's destination is the same, for in no other museum in the world do personal desire and official guidance combine so exactly. Everybody wants to see the Sistine Chapel, the focal point of this almost dreamlike plenty. The distance from the main entrance to the chapel is about half a mile along marble corridors, with some inexplicable twists and turns. The entrance is down a winding staircase with randomly placed windows from which you get unexpected glimpses of the stark walls of the palace, so that you feel you are penetrating deeper and deeper into stone.

Dazzled by galleries filled with jewels and fabrics, parchment and murals, you probably do not realize for the first few seconds that you have actually arrived at the Sistine Chapel. The entrance is through a low door at one side of the altar. Stepping through it can be disconcerting, for the hundreds of faces in the dim light are all looking in your direction. Then you realize that they are staring above you, and you walk a few paces into the chapel, turn round and see that you have entered beneath Michelangelo's fresco of the Last Judgement—just to the right of the terrible figure of Charon, beating the damned out of his boat.

The first impression in the chapel is undeniably of gloom. The windows are set high up in the towering walls, one third of whose height is covered with a painted imitation of drapery. There is a permanent shuffle and susurration from the huge crowd packed together. But this is a place of holiness as well as art, and the weary tourist, sinking gratefully on to the marble steps of the altar, is brought to his feet by a polite but firm admonition. Every so often a strident "*Silenzio!*" will reduce the storm of noise to a whisper; but it shortly rises again. The tourist guides are forbidden to speak above a low voice, but the excited tones of hundreds of people are saying in a dozen languages, "Come and look at this".

All this one records unconsciously before, at last, looking up. After four years' work on the ceiling, Michelangelo's eyes were supposedly so affected that he could read his private correspondence only by holding letters above his head. And after four minutes of gazing at his masterpiece, the visitor is massaging the back of his neck and deploring the Italian penchant for placing great works on that most inaccessible of places, the ceiling.

Besides his famous ceiling, Michelangelo painted the Last Judgement on the eastern wall. The majestic figures in the Judgement—the human body seen as the ultimate in earthly beauty—are unmistakably from the same hand; but here it is as though a veil had been drawn over the luminous mind that had created the figures overhead. Twenty-three years separate the two works, years during which Rome passed from the confidence of the Renaissance to the trauma of the sack by mercenaries in 1527. And even if the outside world had remained serene, the artist's failing health would have drawn the clouds of death over his mind, and coloured his work. He had been 33 when he began the ceiling; he was 56 years old when he started the Last Judgement. Time, too, has placed its mark upon the great mural. Oddly, photography brings it to life, tones down the cracks of naked plaster, lightens the sombre blue. When seen in reality, it appears little more at first than a dull-coloured wall; only on moving closer do the swirling figures stand out—the Christ more preoccupied with cursing the doomed than in welcoming the saved, the macabre horrors of the resurrected corpses, the terror of the damned. The living visitors below are no longer intent on pointing out details, but seem drawn in, mesmerized.

And afterwards, satiated, the visitor looks incuriously upon the gold, blue, and scarlet figures of the side walls, and then glances wearily away while his mind turns to cold drinks and soft seats. But as he does so, he may fleetingly reflect on the glory of this unique city; for those frescos are the creations of the Italian geniuses—Botticelli, Ghirlandaio, Piero della Francesca—any one of whose works elsewhere would be the boasted pride of a nation. Here they can go unnoticed, where there is so much that is grander and greater still. That is the Vatican's greatest treasure of all, and one that is often taken for granted: its permanence. Art may fade, but the Vatican endures, through one changing world after another.

The Lure of Faith

Pilgrims in a tour group follow their leader's rallying symbol, a yellow plastic chrysanthemum, to avoid getting lost in the crowd at St. Peter's basilica.

Each year millions of Roman Catholics turn from everyday tasks and pleasures to undertake a spiritually momentous journey: a pilgrimage to Rome. The tradition is almost as old as the Church. Some 1,500 years ago pilgrims carved their names on catacomb walls, and in the Middle Ages so many came to the city that foreign kings built hostels to house visitors from their countries. In spite of wars, plagues and the Reformation, the practice has increased until today more pilgrims flock to Rome than ever before. Although the trip that once could take a year on foot can now be made in hours by air, a pilgrimage still includes some sacrifice. Besides the expense of travel, the sheer press of numbers demands great devotion, patience and tenacity from pilgrims. But the compensation is mass in St. Peter's—and sometimes even the blessing of the pontiff himself.

Eyes trained on the dais where the Pope will appear, a crowd of pilgrims stands patiently in a drizzle waiting for mass on the feast day of Corpus Christi.

Volunteers gently lead away a nun who has collapsed in St. Peter's Square.

The Pilgrims' Patient Vigil

For outdoor papal masses, pilgrims come early. Pouring from chartered coaches, they pack the vast piazza in front of St. Peter's, and for hours on end they await the man who drew them from all over the earth. At last the noise gives way to quiet, electric anticipation, and the Pope appears before them—a sufficient reward for miles of travel and hours of waiting.

To relive the experience at home, thousands of miles from Rome, a Californian brings along a tape recorder.

An Emotional Moment

For all Catholics a visit to St. Peter's is an emotional experience, but for some—like these Charismatic Catholics from the United States—it can be an ecstatic one. The Charismatics, members of a religious movement founded in America in 1967, throw themselves into the spirit of the occasion with a fervour that can hardly be matched by any other group of pilgrims. Singing and chanting, they become filled by religious emotion.

A Charismatic Catholic, transported by the overwhelming power of her emotions, lifts hands in praise, as a companion stands by, inspired by the Holy Spirit.

Amid a sustained explosion of popping flashbulbs—this multiple-image time exposure was taken with their light—the Pope is borne through St. Peter's on his throne, the sedia gestatoria. Incessantly he bestows his coveted blessing on a throng of waving pilgrims.

The pilgrim's goal is to attend a pontifical mass in the Baroque interior of St. Peter's and to see the Pope himself perform the old ritual beneath Bernini's famous baldacchino. But with the press of numbers in an age of package-tour pilgrimages, only a fraction of the faithful achieve this splendid climax to their journey.

6

"La Bella Figura"

He was a compact man in the prime of life, so broad of shoulder that he seemed to fill the alleyway ahead of me. Earlier, I'd stumbled while crossing a piece of broken ground in the near-darkness, and with one hand he had lifted me to my feet. I was alarmed. What on earth was I doing, penetrating deeper and deeper into unknown lanes accompanied by a total stranger who could break me in two almost without effort? Surely this promise to show me western Rome was a trap; and if it wasn't a trap, what could a labourer know of history and architecture?

But this labourer, it turned out, knew a great deal. We had fallen into conversation earlier that evening in the Campo dei Fiori, and he had been indignant to learn how little I knew of the area of Rome where he had been born. Nothing would satisfy him but that we should start on an exploration, even though it was past 10 o'clock and his work began at six in the morning. By midnight we were still walking and he was still talking, and it seemed that there was nothing else about his home region that I could possibly want to know. He spoke of people dead these 400 years as though they were contemporaries; he had an anecdote for every building, every street corner; shadowy houses took on identity as he described who had lived there—and often enough, who had been killed there. This labourer, whose formal schooling had ended at the age of 12, was an encyclopaedia of lore about his part of Rome. Except for one aspect.

We had returned to the river and paused under one of the graceful plane trees on the bank, motionless in the still night. The name of the tree in Italian had escaped me, and I slapped the trunk and said, "What's the name of this tree?"

He looked at me blankly, then at the tree and back again at me. "Just tree", he said.

"But it must have a proper name."

He shrugged, indifferent. The tree may have had a name but it meant absolutely nothing to him: the entire world of nature was peripheral—irrelevant, almost—to his world, the world of the city.

This reaction to the plane tree provided me with a useful clue to the character of the Roman. He is urban to the core—and perhaps reasonably so, since it was his ancestors who gave the word "urban" to the world. There is, of course, the mass exodus to the country or the beach on Sundays; there are the preposterous "hunting" expeditions when, equipped as for an African safari, the Roman sportsman sallies out into the *Campagna* to kill songbirds. But in general the country to the Roman is merely something that starts where the city stops, a combination of botanical and zoological products that fill a vacuum and provide sustenance or ornament for the city.

A city is the physical expression of the people who built it. The Spartan who boasted that Sparta had no need for walls because each citizen was a brick, uttered a profound truth about the nature of cities. And so Rome, in its baroque exuberance—its statues and gardens, its domes and fountains—is the expression of the Roman. It makes an outright appeal to the senses. Just as the baroque artist of the 17th Century created in stone his mirror of the world, so the ordinary Roman citizen creates an exuberant mirror of his everyday life as a matter of course. This mirror—this idea of himself—he calls *La bella figura.*

But while the artist expressed himself in marble and wood and metal, the citizen's materials are more complex. They comprise clothes and manner, voice and gesture. They go to build the image of himself that he wants to convey—an image in which he himself may come to believe. Thus they permeate every walk of his life. They pervade, and sometimes corrupt, the arts. They even affect politics. And they imply, of course, a particular idea about what a man is or should be.

The phrase, *La bella figura*, like the concept, cannot pass into another language without becoming modified. Literally, perhaps, it could be translated as "the beautiful figure", but it certainly doesn't mean that and is, if anything, more applicable to males than females. "Cutting a dash" comes closer, except for its jazzy overtones. "Face"? Perhaps, but face has a negative quality: the essence of preserving face is not to lose it, while to attain and maintain *La bella figura* is an achievement as positive, as desirable, as running the four-minute-mile or playing a Chopin study. All Italians possess the desire; the Romans raise its practice to the status of an art—a dramatic art played out on a 2,000-year-old stage where there is a scenario for every nuance.

La bella figura has something to do with snobbery, but nothing to do with class: the impoverished nobleman will put himself deeper into debt in order to maintain two bored and idle servants in his house; the labourer's wife will skimp the family spaghetti to ensure that her small daughter is dressed in uncomfortable finery on Sunday.

Above all, *La bella figura* has to do with a man's approach to women (and vice versa). For women are not only the targets for much of his bravura; they are also, subtly, its creators. From the day he becomes aware of himself as a personality, the Roman boy knows that the women in his life— mothers and sisters alike—exist to serve him and that in time some fortunate girl will take up the divinely-appointed role of his wife. First, though, he must attract her and impress her. Most of the girls, of all classes, accept it; it is difficult, after all, to transcend the society of which one is part. I discussed the matter once with a young wife who, although Roman born, had

The concept of La bella figura long ago rooted itself in the ecclesiastical dress of Roman prelates. This cardinal in lacy choir robes, which are worn to all official church functions, imposes his own touch of style by riding in the front seat of the car, next to his driver.

spent her formative years in England. "I'm not expected to be just his servant, but his mother," she said—"not merely waiting on him, bringing him what he wants, but anticipating him so that the want is satisfied, even before he formulates it in his own mind." With this background of worshipful womenfolk, it is perhaps inevitable that the Roman male should turn towards histrionics as his prime means of self-expression.

For both sexes dress and manner are vital. Matter is more important than mind. In Rome I was struck again and again by a sense of living out a play. The baroque scenery of spectacular but sometimes rather stagy buildings was inhabited by people to whom, likewise, appearance seemed to be of paramount importance.

This concern with outward effect, of course, reaches its zenith in clothes. Both men and women dress with a kind of careful spontaneity. Long before the rest of Europe decided to go casual the Roman male repudiated that dreary example of correct dress—the three-piece suit—and walked out in a well-cut, figure-hugging shirt, open to show a manly chest and gold medallion. Casual strollers or bank clerks, adolescents or paterfamilias, nearly all dress in these clinging shirts and trousers. The tightness of the trousers produced another sartorial novelty: it is quite impossible for a Roman male to carry keys or money, matches or cigarettes, in the pockets of his beautifully-cut trousers. He has therefore adopted what is, in effect, a handbag—a leather envelope dangling from a wrist strap—for previous generations the badge of the female.

The young unmarried women, and the women of more leisured classes, have a dress and a freedom of manner that can cause misunderstandings on the part of uninitiated northerners. The Roman women's clothes are more colourful than those, for instance, of the northern Italian. The ungallant might, perhaps, describe the typical Roman woman as dumpy, the gallant as generously endowed, if a little on the short side. Either way, she makes the most of her God-given figure. The mini-skirt never caught on here, as it did in the North—not because it was immodest but because it didn't flatter the shorter Roman leg. The girls took to figure-hugging trousers with enthusiasm, however, and are not shy of wearing revealing clothes; while platform shoes became popular because they increased height. Unashamed use of tanning lamps enables women to trip out into early spring sunlight already deeply bronzed, and as summer progresses, more and more items of clothing are discarded, including stockings.

This physical aspect of *La bella figura* goes back to ancient times. Early Romans were even buried with all their jewellery, often with toilet boxes, hairpins, cosmetics, and sponges. Their women's "foundation cream" was made by dissolving lead in vinegar to make a paste that was then spread over face, shoulders and arms to give them a fashionable chalky-white appearance. Wine dregs and ochre produced a red variant of the same paste for lips and cheeks; antimony was used for blacking lashes; and Ovid even sings the praises of a "halcyon cream", to clear up spots on the skin, made from pulverized bird droppings.

As for the men, they were not always satisfied by shaving with primitive bronze and iron razors. A cleaner look was obtained by singeing off hairs or by removing them with a mixture of pitch, resin, goat's bile or donkey grease. They even depilated their legs by the same processes, although it was sometimes considered a sign of effeminacy.

The rules governing *La bella figura* are in part the product of the Italian's passionate love of beauty. Peter Nichols succinctly makes the point in his book *Italia, Italia.* "There is no limit to the value placed by most Italians on physical beauty. A beautiful woman or a handsome man are immediately admired for their good looks and elegance: and there the matter stops. No other qualities or defects are worth worrying about if physical beauty is evident.... It is of no account that he might be greedy, or selfish, or kind, or intelligent, or thoughtful or sulky."

Such is the view of a sympathetic foreign observer. Luigi Barzini, as an Italian, ponders this national trait which is so typically Roman. "The show is as important as, many times more important than, reality. This is perhaps due to the fact that the climate has allowed Italians to live mostly outside their houses, in the streets and *piazze.* . . . Or because they are naturally inclined towards arranging a spectacle, acting a character, staging a drama; or because they are most pleased by display than others, to the point that they do not countenance life when it is reduced to unadorned truth." The ten-day Lenten carnival, which was once pre-eminently the dramatization of everyday life, is now a dull echo of the old days. But much time, effort and money is still expended on making *La bella figura* with the children's costumes. Families who live in modest apartments will spend the equivalent of a month's rent to fit out their youngsters as "Zorro" and the "Blue Fairy" for the carnival, walking the children up and down the main street of their district with admonition not to run or kick because they might dirty their costumes.

All in all, *La bella figura* is most obviously expressed through dress; and it was not long before I encountered the phenomenon personally. For it is by means of his dress that a stranger is categorized. I discovered this in a practical demonstration while tramping around Rome day after day for this book. I developed a system; one day I might be visiting some high official behind his wall of secretaries, and the next I might be trudging through a sewer or scrambling over ruins. So I evolved two different uniforms. The one, while laying no claim to elegance, was neat and included proper shoes, a jacket and tie. The other was shabby—baggy trousers, sandals and a windcheater with useful, voluminous pockets. It did not take me long to discover that if I wanted to achieve anything, I must never wear the wrong uniform in the wrong place or at the wrong time. For, to the

In hats decorated with saucer-sized brass badges and cascades of tail feathers from cockerels, soldiers of a regiment of riflemen march through Rome.

The Splendid Soldiers

Feathers may seem an unlikely adornment for tough riflemen like those above, but such a uniform is not the most flamboyant to be seen in Rome during an Armed Forces Day parade, as the following pages demonstrate. The Italians—and the Romans in particular—have sometimes been accused of setting more store by appearance than by substance, and their appetite for show is amply illustrated here. War in Italy in the Renaissance was (in the words of Luigi Barzini) "an elegant pantomime" with "beautiful props, flags, coloured tents, caparisoned horses, rolls of drums"—and few casualties. Nowadays, though Italy does not rely on *La bella figura* for her defence, her men in uniform still display the dress and panache to satisfy the Roman love of a grand martial show.

In plumes, cockades and fringed epaulettes these carabinieri may resemble the cast of a Gilbert and Sullivan operetta, with expressions to match (above), but they are active members of a modern police force. Administratively part of the Italian Army, carabinieri cherish their right to parade on Armed Forces Day.

Proud and serious, Officer Cadets of the Military Academy at Modena show watching Romans their paces—and the navy blue and crimson finery of their uniforms.

Romans, my appearance was everything. When I was dressed shabbily I at once became a target for the propaganda of the earnest young Communists who haunted the Piazza Navona and Campo dei Fiori. But beggars and waiters ignored me, and it proved difficult for me to penetrate beyond the waiting rooms of government offices. But in my necktied and jacketed splendour I found that the young Communists ignored me, that beggars made themselves a nuisance, and that the higher levels of bureaucracy were immediately accessible.

The importance of appearances—of the visual and the sensual—has pervaded all the arts. Sometimes it has even marred them. The actor Orson Welles is credited with the unkind but perspicacious remark that the only bad actors in Italy are to be found among the professionals. "After all," a young Roman lawyer once remarked to me with a touch of complacency, "what have we ever produced throughout history except priests, lawyers and actors? And priests and lawyers are merely taking part in another kind of drama."

Apart from opera—and even that is better in Milan—Rome's formal theatre offers no more than an opportunity for social display. But, as if in indignant response, the informal theatre—the so-called "underground theatre"—is filled with vivid life. Throughout the city small companies pack young audiences into cramped little rooms that would bring tears to the eyes of a fire chief. And if you drift around the Campo dei Fiori or the Piazza Navona long enough, you will see some political activist putting on an open-air show that would cost a substantial sum if produced professionally. The activists are usually extreme Left Wing, partly because the Right still lies under the shadow of the Thirties and partly because radical Socialism or Communism can be a disguise for the rebellious element that has plagued the city rulers century after century.

Certainly the Left seems to have an inexhaustible pool of dramatic talent to draw upon. I was in the Campo dei Fiori once when three young people set up shop with a minimum of equipment and gripped the attention of an audience for half an hour, in spite of the presence of a large number of grim-looking police. One young man was a guitarist and ballad singer, the other a ragged Worker, while the girl was the Wicked Capitalist, made up with a Dracula face. Their ancestors would have staged a similar drama with Sin or Death as the villain, and their even remoter forebears would have garnished the whole with a sacrifice.

This flair for theatrical display, the natural upshot of *La bella figura*, seems to be most dramatic at political rallies. One evening in the Piazza Navona I was startled to see a forest of blood-red Communist banners rise up against the honey-coloured stone, and by nightfall the stage was set for what I expected to be a speech-making. But it was not so. The crowds thickened, most of them casual Sunday strollers. Then, without warning, without political exhortation, without a single overworked cliché to introduce it, music filled the square. For nearly two hours guitarist succeeded singer, drummer succeeded accordionist, flute succeeded bagpipe.

The pace never flagged, only the emotion changing: now the songs were martial, now tragic, now sorrowful, now triumphant. I suspect that the majority of the tunes were traditional, some probably as old as the square itself, and that these youthful idealists had plundered the songs born of a capitalist society to decorate their Utopia. For these two hours the crowd reacted as if it were itself an enormous musical instrument, and responded unashamedly in the Latin manner that can soften even protest and rebellion with a human warmth.

All this ferment of emotion and display is acted out against a backdrop that is entirely suitable. For the Baroque architecture of Rome also embodied its propaganda—a Christian one—in the most graceful and human shapes. This is *La bella figura* in stone. It is like nothing so much as beautiful stage scenery. And it can be no coincidence that the Baroque was born here. For centuries the city had drawn on the inspiration of other people, but when it evolved its own form of expression it created this rich, convoluted and totally artificial world.

Baroque is an attitude of mind, and a manner as well as an art style; for it covers not only music and painting but even everyday speech. It appeared during the 17th Century, transformed Rome into a fantasy, then disappeared. The 19th Century was contemptuous of its frivolity, and only during our own day has it returned to favour.

Yet Baroque is not all hyperbole and over-richness. Its badge in Rome is Francesco Borromini's Church of S. Ivo in the courtyard of the Palazzo della Sapienza. From a distance the tower of S. Ivo might be called *La bellissima figura* in Baroque architecture; indeed to the irreverent it resembles an enormous confectionery swirled round with cream and topped off with a cherry. But on closer inspection the most determined detractor cannot but respect the skill with which Borromini integrated his church into a building that already existed, making it appear as though the building were added to the church instead of vice versa. And inside S. Ivo's there is harmony and restraint. Over-indulgence in gilt, the besetting sin of the Baroque, has been avoided: it is a white interior, with gold used only as punctuation; and nobody since has swamped the interior with flattering cherubs or drooping garlands.

Borromini is to Rome what Sir Christopher Wren is to London: the man who placed the stamp of his day upon an ancient city. Looked at from any vantage point, the skyline of old Rome is largely the skyline wrought by Borromini in the mid-17th Century. And if Borromini provided the setting, so his contemporary and rival, Bernini, filled in the details. Bernini practised as architect, too: his ornate but beautifully-proportioned church of S. Andrea al Quirinale goes some way to make Baroque acceptable to the

The two battered classical figures above, nicknamed Pasquino (right) and Babuino— "Baboon"—(left), are among several monuments on which Roman wits of the past used to stick caustic political epigrams. Referred to as "talking statues", they afforded a traditional outlet for anonymous comment during periods when autocratic regimes muzzled criticism.

more sober minded. Still, it is as a sculptor that he remains in the memory— and as a master of theatre. For what else but a stage is the vast Piazza of St. Peter's, embraced by Bernini's colonnade, or the Piazza Navona, with his Fountain of the Rivers, where everything seems to be happening at once? The Scala Regia—the formal entrance to the Vatican—is overtly theatrical, with the illusion of a long perspective created by shortening the columns and placing them closer together, as they ascend the staircase. So too is the Bridge of Sant'Angelo, thronged with angels and saints carrying the symbols of the Passion. The statues that overlook the Piazza of St. Peter's; the swooning St. Theresa; the dramatic portrait busts—all give an impression of supreme energy and abundance.

But just as it is easy to criticize the Baroque for its theatricality, so it is simple to think of *La bella figura* as pure display. All this gesture and swagger, this self-flourishing—is it anything more than a façade? Surely it is. *La bella figura* reflects what the inner person desires to be. It expresses the striving towards a familiar Renaissance ideal—the man who is equal to all things. It has to do with thinking on one's feet, with the ability to adapt and adopt. As he lay dying, Pope John XXIII chided those around him for their sorrowful appearance. "Come, tell me a joke: I think I can last that long." In this composure he showed himself to be a good adopted Roman, for a Roman would hope to find something witty to say whether he was standing outside the gates of heaven or hell.

At the same time, Pope John's humour betrayed his "foreign" origins, for it was warm, compassionate and self-critical, whereas true Roman wit is

Nuns in their black-and-white habits tend a flock of demure Roman girls dressed by their mothers in expensive costumes made at home for Corpus Christi.

In nun's habit, a child strikes a worldly pose, her slacks showing beneath.

mordant, cruel and always directed outwards. It is also strongly anti-establishment. Examples span the centuries. When the austere Pope Adrian VI died in 1523, bouquets with the legend "the deliverer of Rome" were laid outside the door of his physician. Today the letters S.C.V. (*Stato Cittá del Vaticano*) which appear on the sleek black cars of the Diplomatic Corps are humorously translated as "*Se Cristo Vedesse*" (If Christ could only see).

The sharp Roman tongue is rivalled in other cities—in particular by the wits of Florence—but Rome is unique in finding expression for this wit in the shape of its "talking statues". These were adapted to the ancient art of graffiti, for it became the custom for malcontents to write their witticisms upon several well-known statues in the city. The earliest and most popular was the so-called statue of Pasquino: indeed, the genre took its name from him, and any placard or poster criticism soon became known in Rome as a "pasquinade".

The statue of Pasquino was once part of a classical group that probably stood in the Stadium of Domitian, now the Piazza Navona. Bernini considered it to be the finest surviving antique sculpture, mutilated though it is. It was set up in the tiny square near the Piazza Navona soon after it was discovered in 1501, and almost immediately the scurrilous comments appeared. The first recorded epigram seems to have been inspired by the simony of Pope Alexander VI.

Alexander sells the keys, the altar, Christ Himself.

He has a right to—he bought them.

Thereafter, year by year and century after century, the little slips of paper with their scribbled lampoons, usually in the form of Latin puns, appeared on the statue. Most were aimed at Rome's all-powerful rulers, the popes. Urban VIII, the Barberini Pope who plundered the classical city to build his own grandiose monuments, awoke one morning to find that Pasquino had declared: "*Quod non fecerunt barbari, fecerunt Barberini*" (What the barbarians didn't do, the Barberini did). The squib was brought up to date in the 1930s when great chunks of Rome were being gouged out by Mussolini's architects for triumphal avenues and archaeological display. "*Quod non fecerunt Barberini, fecit Mussolini*". Innocent X's sister-in-law Olimpia was satirized skilfully as "*Olim pia, nunc impia*" ("Once pious, now impious"). When the French, in their turn, plundered Rome on behalf of Napoleon Bonaparte, Pasquino made a pun that is still current: "*I Francesi son tutti ladri. Non tutti—ma buona parte*" (The French are all thieves. Not all—but most).

Most of the pasquinades were the work of scholarly hands, and today most of them seem musty and contrived. But at the same time, if they did not cut a figure they were capable of driving their victim to the quick. The virtuous but pedantic Dutchman, Pope Adrian VI, goaded to fury by Pasquino's sneers, ordered the statue to be broken up and thrown into the river. But a cardinal warned him: "Each piece will become a talking frog", and Adrian wisely changed his mind.

For a while there was even a dialogue of the statues! It became customary for Pasquino's epigrams to be elaborated, or the rhetorical questions answered, the following morning, on the immense statue of Marforio, which was part of an ancient fountain that had stood at the foot of the Capitol. But an irritated authority removed Marforio to the courtyard of the Capitoline Museum and put an end to this escalation of satire. So the story goes, anyway. In any case, now, while Pasquino stands dusty and tortured in an unimpressive square, Marforio sprawls at ease before a beautiful fountain in a cool courtyard.

Marforio and Pasquino provided the best-known opportunities for verbal use of *La bella figura*. But from time to time other Roman statues served a similar function for their immediate localities. During the Fascist era, when disastrous attempts were made to find substitutes for the ingredients of bread, one of the iron-hard loaves was placed at the foot of the statue of Julius Caesar on the Via dei Fori Imperiali. The notice with it read: "You who are made of bronze and with a belly of lead—see if you can eat this."

Such saucy commentary—the essence of *La bella figura*—is perhaps the city's strongest guardian against inhumane political systems. And while *La bella figura* may often be a shallow phenomenon, theatrical, childish, even depraved, it is always warm and open. It expresses man's heart rather than his mind. It is the cry of the individual refusing to be drowned by the roar of the crowd or of the state. And so it offers assurance for the future that when ideologies grow monstrous in their demands, other Pasquinos and Marforios will arise, and will carry the old messages of healthy irreverence and sturdy independence—with a Roman style and flair all their own.

The Celestial Ceilings

The shallow dome of S. Carlo alle Quattro Fontane is made to look deeper than it is because its geometric shapes gradually diminish in size towards the top.

The Baroque is Rome's own style. It flowered there in the early 17th Century when native genius and papal patronage fused to create a powerful, emotive art. By the early 18th Century, it had spread to Germany and as far as South America. In Rome its greatest practitioners were Borromini and Bernini. Their churches, although small, express the drama of Roman Baroque, lifting the eye and the heart to magnificent ceilings like the examples on these pages. The Church of S. Carlo alle Quattro Fontane, finished in 1641, the interior of whose dome is seen above, was the first major work by Borromini. The church encompasses an area no larger than one of the piers that supports the dome of St. Peter's; yet the oval ceiling, coffered in a honeycomb of geometric shapes and flooded with white light, conveys a sensation of spacious grandeur.

The star-studded sides of S. Ivo alla Sapienza's star-shaped dome converge on a circle of still more stars.

Borromini's Starry Heights

Borromini, like the ancient Romans, based his architecture on principles of pure geometry. For the church of S. Ivo alla Sapienza (right), commissioned by Pope Urban VIII and built between 1642 and 1650, he chose a six-pointed star for his ground-plan and carried the shape up into the dome (above). Its harmonious interior marks it as the masterpiece of this inspired architect—who was however a depressed, sickly man. He killed himself in 1667.

Gold around the altar gleams in the dome's bright light and contrasts with the church's simple white decoration of papal crowns, wreaths, stars and angels.

Ringing the skylight of S. Andrea al Quirinale, winged cherubs look down at earth. Above them the Dove of the Holy Ghost is enclosed within a circle of light.

Bernini's Golden Portals

Bernini—a sculptor and painter, as well as architect—is synonymous with Baroque. His lifetime (1598-1680) spanned Baroque's golden age. A flamboyant genius who began working in marble at the age of eight, Bernini in 1658 designed S. Andrea al Quirinale with a sculptor's eye. All attention is drawn to the gilded dome (right), lavish with ornament and lit from above so that its central opening suggests a symbolic entrance to heaven.

A coffered dome spreads like a tent over the main body of the church, while a smaller, pillared dome—surrounded by the rays of a sunburst—lights the altar.

7

Strangers in Residence

On the left bank of the river, less than a mile from the Colosseum, rises the green and shapely mass of the Aventine Hill. Southernmost of the original Seven Hills, it lay outside the *pomerium* or semi-mystical religious boundary of ancient Rome throughout the Republican era (509-27 B.C.). Under the later Empire it became a sparsely populated aristocratic quarter, site of the homes and palaces of rulers. Even now it is a lightly-occupied retreat near the monumental heart of Rome. The roads that cross it seem more like country lanes than urban streets: in autumn they are wreathed in woodsmoke and the vines hang heavy with fruit. A cobbled lane climbs steeply from the Tiber. At the hill-crest it passes through an archway and emerges on to a level space, a formal walled garden planted with orange trees and edged with a parapet from which the land drops sheer for a hundred feet and more to the river.

This is the Parco Savello, opened to the public in 1932 on the site of a 12th-Century fortress of the Savelli family. But this quiet hillside always carries me back in time much further than that and, in doing so, focuses my alien mind on one of the city's most uncompromising traits: its insularity. For long before the Savelli fortress was built here, the spot was occupied by a palace built by a youthful German emperor, Otto III, whose poignant story epitomizes the fate of most foreigners in Rome.

As every European language records in its own way, all roads lead to Rome. Down the centuries pilgrims, scholars, rulers, merchants, artists, migrants and tourists have come in millions. Although most are transients, with no interest in belonging, there have always been those who conceived a passion to stay. Rome's power lies not only in attracting but in holding, so that those who come for a week or a month may stay for a year or a life-time. But of those who have remained, few have truly become part of the city. Some, like the English, are insular, perhaps in self-defence: others, like the Germans and, more lately, the Americans, immerse themselves in their new-found home only to discover that they cannot become truly Roman. The foreigner remains forever foreign.

It is sometimes a sad awakening. A sense of rejection and betrayal follows: "I was ready to give so much", the foreigner mumbles, forgetting that the city is satiated, after all those years and all those millions of visitors, with foreigners. Eventually the resident *straniero* comes to look on the whole matter with much the same detached and cynical air with which Romans themselves view life—and in this they both at least show an affinity. The foreigner knows that even Italians from other parts of Italy seldom are

Thronged as usual with a milling crowd, the Spanish Steps are a favourite rendezvous, especially for foreigners. Begun in 1723 and completed three years later, the steps are called Spanish because the 17th-Century palazzo of the Spanish ambassador to the Vatican is situated in the Piazza di Spagna below.

absorbed into Rome: after years of residence in the city, they are still identified as "Mrs. Rossi from Turin", or "Neapolitan Maria" and if in the end the foreigner is still in need of consolation, all he has to do is think of what happened to Vittorio Emanuele who had done so much to unite Italy. Upon taking up residence in the Quirinal Palace, the traditional residence of Italy's rulers, the King was enthusiastically greeted by a large crowd. He embarked on a rousing address, but in the middle of it, the noonday gun went off and the crowd began to disperse until only a few people were left. The King asked a minister for an explanation of their behaviour. "They've heard it all", he said. "What do you expect from a people who heard Cicero speak?"

There is no more tragic example of the foreigner who tried to become a Roman than that of Otto III. Otto's grandfather, Otto I, was the true founder of the Holy Roman Empire, re-establishing in 962 the authority conferred by Pope Leo on Charlemagne in 800. He and his son, Otto II, came as near as was possible to subduing the unruly Romans by force. Otto III, ascending to the imperial throne in 996 at the age of 15, determined to try peaceful methods.

Surprisingly for one so young, he seemed well qualified for the task. He hated Germany and much preferred Rome. He had become something of an intellectual prodigy (he was nicknamed "The Wonder of the World") under a French astronomer-mathematician, Gerbert of Aurillac. And his political ideas were suitably inspiring: he wanted to restore to Rome its full imperial glory and authority.

In pursuit of this goal, he appointed as Pope his venerable and agreeable tutor. He built a palace on the Aventine Hill, declared Rome to be once again *Caput Mundi*, the capital of the world, and established complex and colourful rituals to amaze and inspire his subjects. He dressed in gold, wore a ceremonial robe decorated with 365 bells (one for each day of the year), had visitors prostrate themselves in his presence and declared himself supreme both temporally and spiritually, as "the Servant of Jesus Christ" and "the Consul of the Roman Senate and People".

The Romans were not impressed. They thought his venerable and agreeable tutor was a magician, and they distrusted Otto's mixture of Latin, Christian and Germanic ritual. In 1001 they revolted and penned him up in his palace. He appealed to them in a curiously moving speech, which reveals that he never really understood what he was up against. "Are you my Romans? For love of you I have abandoned my own Saxons and Germans, my own blood." The Romans, who have seldom shown extremes of either gratitude or xenophobia, did not kill him. They simply let him leave the city, with his Pope. Otto summoned reinforcements from Germany, but he died, exhausted, some months later, within sight of his beloved, inhospitable Rome, before the reinforcements could reach him. He was not quite 22 years old.

Bright sunshine casts the lofty, coffered ceiling of the Arch of Titus into shadow and illuminates the carved relief on its side. The arch, dominating the eastern end of the Forum, commemorates the capture of Jerusalem in A.D. 70 by Titus, the emperor Trajan's elder son. The relief depicts the spoils of Jerusalem, among them the seven-branched candlestick from the great temple of the Jews.

A little less than a mile upstream from the Aventine Hill lies the Jewish ghetto, an area that characterizes equally clearly, and over rather a longer period, the relationship between foreigners and their adopted city. There have been Jews in Rome for more than 2,000 years. By and large, they escaped the persecutions to which their Eastern European brethren were routinely subjected, thanks to Rome's way with foreigners: they were grudgingly tolerated, occasionally humiliated, but never totally rejected.

Nor were they ever totally accepted. Jews first arrived in Rome in 61 B.C., as enslaved prisoners-of-war from Jerusalem in the train of the victorious general Pompey. They bought their freedom with ransom money raised by half-starving themselves and selling their corn ration. There was another influx of slaves in A.D. 70 when Titus took Jerusalem, and thousands of Jews were brought to labour on the Colosseum. Those too bought their freedom, and the small Jewish colony swelled to become an established, if barely tolerated, part of Rome.

Throughout history certain ceremonies and occasional outbursts of prejudice, usually from the Roman mob, underlined this ambiguous relationship. In the Middle Ages, during papal coronations, the papal procession would halt near the Jewish quarter on its way to the Lateran palace. The Jewish leaders would offer the sacred scrolls of the Pentateuch, which the Pope would bless. In 1215 it was decreed that all Jews and heretics must wear a circle of yellow cloth upon their breasts; and during the Renaissance Eugenius IV forbade all Christians to trade with Jews, or to engage in any form of social intercourse with them.

Under Paul II in the 15th Century, public sport was made of the Jews by forcing some to eat a heavy meal and then run in carnival races. As late as 1667 a guide to Rome noted that during these races "the asses ran first, then the Jews, naked, with only a band around the loins, then the buffaloes, then the Barbary horses". Clement IX modified the custom the following year: the victims were allowed to pay a heavy fine to avoid racing.

Until the 18th Century it was the custom on the first Saturday of *Carnevale* for the Jewish leaders to pay homage to the city fathers at the Capitol. Throwing themselves on their knees, they offered flowers and 20 *scudi* to ornament the balcony in which the Roman Senate sat. They then appeared before the chief senator and implored permission to remain in Rome. The senator would place his foot on their foreheads, then order them to stand up, and reply that Jews were not adopted in Rome but allowed from compassion to remain there. Even after this humiliating ceremony was abandoned, Jews continued to go to the Capitol to offer tribute as late as the 19th Century.

It was the austere and temperamental Pope Paul IV, a driving force behind the 16th-Century Roman Inquisition, who first enclosed the Jews in a ghetto. Implacably opposed to all supposed enemies of Catholicism, he justified his action by accepting the age-old slander that all Jews must bear the collective guilt for deicide. "It is most absurd and unsuitable", ran the papal Bull establishing the ghetto, "that the Jews, whose own crime has plunged them into everlasting slavery, should presume to dwell and mix with Christians." By enclosing them, Paul IV intended their humiliation. Unwittingly, he did them a service. Behind the high walls of the ghetto into which they were forced on July 26, 1555, the Jews escaped the threat of harm at the hands of their Roman neighbours and were able to go about their affairs in peace.

Peace, but not comfort. They were crowded into a narrow space, and earned their living as best they could, in various unexpected ways. The finest doctors were nearly always Jewish, and many a pope turned a blind eye to the presence of a medical deicide in the precincts of the Vatican. In addition, some turned to magic: since Jews were, according to the teaching of the Church, already damned to hell, they could practise the trade of witchcraft with impunity, and a furtive trickle of Christian figures visited Jewish necromancers in the ghetto. But in the main, Jewish livelihood was gained through trade in old clothes, an occupation that turned the area into one of the sights of the city. When travelling became fashionable in the 19th Century, a visit to the ghetto was one of the fixed points of a Roman tour, and visiting writers left their descriptions of the ferment within the walls.

"On entering the Ghetto", wrote the 19th-Century German historian Ferdinand Gregorovius, "we see Israel in full restless labour and activity. The people sit in their doorways, or outside in the streets, which receive hardly more light than the damp and gloomy chambers, and grub in their old trumpery, or patch and sew diligently. It is inexpressible what a chaos of shreds and patches is here accumulated. The fragments lie in heaps before the doors, gold fringes, scraps of silk brocade, bits of velvet, red patches, blue patches, orange, yellow, black and white, torn old, slashed and tattered pieces, large and small. The Jews might mend up all creation with it, and patch the whole world as gainly as a harlequin's coat. It is chiefly in the Fiumara, the street lying lowest and nearest to the river, that this business is carried on. I have often seen, with a feeling of pain, the pale, stooping, starving figures, laboriously plying the needle, men as well as women, girls and children. Misery stares forth from their tangled hair."

This was in the middle of the 19th Century. Yet within 50 years the ghetto boundaries had almost all disappeared. The entire western section was torn down at the turn of the century, as part of the reconstruction that followed the unification of Italy in 1870. But the spirit of the ghetto still lingers in some small, dark corners. If you approach the area from the city centre, for instance, you go along the narrow Via della Reginella, one of the few surviving streets of the old ghetto. Overhung by houses and gloomy even in daylight, it is oppressive enough to suggest the misery that once had dwelled there.

Today's Jews in Rome are not confined to the ghetto; they are prominent in the city's intellectual circles and dominate commerce in fabrics, clothes, silverware and jewellery. And they have forged bonds of understanding and friendship with other Romans. When the wife of a leading jeweller was killed recently in a restaurant hold-up, many of the non-Jewish shops around her husband's shut down in mourning. In 1956 when a rekindling of Fascist sentiments was occasioned by the rise of a Right Wing political party, a synagogue was desecrated, the altar defiled and slogans were painted on the steps by a few vandals. But the rabbi who had come to reconsecrate the temple found a bank of huge wreaths from Roman citizens expressing their regrets and sympathy.

This change in attitude can be traced back partly to the war. In the beginning the Nazis left the Jews alone. But in October 1943 their attitude hardened. The head of the Gestapo received orders from Berlin to deport all Jews deemed enemies of the Nazis. Troops could not be spared for the round-up, however, and the order was transmuted into a demand for ransom: if the Jews did not come up with 50 kilos of gold in 36 hours, 200 of them would be deported. The Jewish community hurriedly organized the collection. Once, when it looked as if the goal of 50 kilos could not be achieved, an appeal was made to the Vatican. Pope Pius XII authorized a loan; but it was not needed. Contributions from non-Jews fulfilled the goal. One who watched the scene described it: "cautiously, as if fearing a refusal, or intimidated by the idea of offering gold to rich Jews, some 'Aryans' presented themselves. They entered the room adjacent to the synagogue in an awkward fashion, not knowing if they should take off their hats or keep their heads covered, as is commonly known to be Jewish ritual use. Almost humbly they asked if they too could . . . if it would be acceptable . . . unfortunately they did not leave their names."

Three weeks later, on 16 October 1943, Nazi troops rounded up 1,050 Jews and deported them to Auschwitz, where one week later most of them died in the gas chamber. Only 15 returned to Rome. Today there are 15,000 Jews in Rome, 3,000 more than were there before the war. In the 2,000 years that Jews have lived in Rome, they have formed one of the world's most stable Jewish communities; and the people who make it up have the distinction of being among the oldest "Romans".

The ghetto was forced upon its inhabitants. The Anglo-Saxon ghetto near the Spanish Steps evolved in response to the wishes of its once-wealthy residents. Although the glory has departed with milord and his coaches and the British today are far down in the league of big spenders, it is still possible for an English-speaking tourist to leave Rome convinced that its true heart beats in the pricy teashops and fashion houses of the Via Condotti and the Corso.

Anglo-Saxons have often remained remote, quixotically combining extravagant and uncritical praise with a sturdy refusal to learn the language or to penetrate behind the façade. To do that would be to risk going native. The young English dandies of the Grand Tour may have displayed sufficient foreign mannerisms on their return home to infuriate their relatives and friends, but while actually abroad they affected the most insular English manners. Perhaps it was better to appear to reject Rome than to accept the reality of being rejected by Rome.

An English periodical carried a fictional letter that parodied this attitude. "Here are a great many agreeable English gentlemen", writes a son to his father from Rome. "We are about nine or ten as smart bucks as any in England. We constantly breakfast together, and then go either to see the sights, or drive about the outskirts of Rome in chaises. We meet before dinner at the English coffee-house where there is a very good billiard table and very good company. From thence we go and dine together by turns at each other's lodgings. Then after a cheerful glass of claret, for we have made a shift to get some here, we go to the coffee-house again, from thence to supper and so to bed. I do not believe these Romans are a bit like the old Romans. They are a parcel of thin-gutted snivelling, cringing dogs and I verily believe that our set could thrash forty of them. We never go among them. It would not be worth while: besides which, we none of us speak Italian and none of those signors speak English which shows what sort of fellows they are."

All foreigners are attracted to the Spanish Steps, but the English have always had a particularly close attachment to the area. Keats died in a house at the foot of the Steps, a fact that has made this corner of this particular foreign field forever England, at least for the English. English travellers have again and again commented on the Steps. Charles Dickens was particularly venomous about the artists' models who haunted the Steps in his day: "The first time I went up there I could not conceive why the faces seemed so familiar to me. . . . I soon found that we had made acquaintance, and improved it, for several years on the walls of various Exhibition Galleries. There is one old gentleman, with long white hair and an immense beard, who, to my knowledge, has gone half through the catalogue of the Royal Academy. This is the venerable, or patriarchal model. . . . There is another man in a blue cloak who always pretends to be asleep in the sun. . . . This is the *dolce far niente* model. There is another man in a brown cloak, who leans against a wall, with his arms folded in his mantle, and looks out of the corner of his eyes; which are just visible beneath the broad slouched hat. This is the assassin model. . . . As to Domestic Happiness, and Holy Families, they should come very cheap, for there are lumps of them all up the Steps; and the cream of the thing, is, that they are all the falsest vagabonds. . . . " The models may have disappeared, but many who show up here today still seem as interested in being seen as in the old days, and among them are some whose particular passion is preying on the tourist. *continued on page 162*

A light burns over a relief of the Holy Family; below is a chalked message: "Beware of the dog Edmondo".

Neighbourhood Piety

The daily faith of the devout Catholics who still make up a large part of Rome's population is expressed in the multitude of small shrines, usually no more than plaques or niches, that an observant traveller will see on street walls throughout the city. This is an unassuming faith, with none of the papacy's cosmopolitan splendour. Before many of the little shrines an electric light stands in for a votive candle, and an artificial flower or two may add a spot of colour. Some may boast a timeworn carving, but more often their images are fairly recent: a mosaic or a ceramic reproduction of a renaissance relief. Their unceremonious conjunction in the crowded streetscape with signs of every sort does nothing to dispel the simple and touching piety they express.

A coin inserted in a slot lights an electric candle to the Madonna of Divine Love in the Piazzale Brazile. She is Rome's own Madonna, with more than 60 shrines.

With stark effect, a small ceramic plaque of the Virgin and Child and a large sign advertising quick food are arbitrarily juxtaposed on a dun-coloured wall.

AVE O MARIA

A glowing lantern leans across a figurine of Jesus in a simple wall niche.

An alcove harbours a Renaissance-style Madonna and Child with angels.

Other foreigners, besides the English, make themselves at home in the area around the Spanish Steps, and always have. The near-by *Caffé Greco*, on the Via Condotti, used to be the favourite meeting place of famous visiting artists. Wagner, Goethe, Byron, Gogol, Strindberg, Ibsen, all have passed through its doors. A watercolour of the *Caffé* painted in 1842 shows it as a cosy inn peopled by well-to-do "bohemians". The Germans were particularly fond of it, as Mendelssohn, who himself had a house on the Spanish Steps, recorded with distaste. "It is a small, dark room, about 25 feet wide where you may smoke on one side but not the other. They sit around it on benches, with sombreros on their heads and huge mastiffs beside them. They puff fearful clouds of smoke and hurl abuse at one another... drink their coffee and talk of Titian and Pordenone just as if they were sitting next to them, wearing beards and sou'westers like theirs. Moreover, they paint such sickly Madonnas, such feeble saints and suchlike milksop heroes and I long to have a go at them."

The *Caffé* has been tidied up now, and looks rather more like a licensed teashop than a robustious tavern. Almost certainly it is not so much used by poets and artists as by those waiting for the poets and artists to turn up, or by the beautiful expensive youths of Rome, come to show off their beautiful and expensive clothes to one another. But the crimson plush-covered chairs are good to sink into and the drinks are cold and strong and even here one can sit happily for hours alone or, as part of a party.

So thoroughly foreign is the area that the sound of Italian on the streets sometimes seems a rarity. Certainly this can be true in the shops, fashionable places that cater to foreigners. It has not escaped the ever-cynical attention of the Romans that the great experiment in cleansing the city of its plague of traffic began in this favoured quarter. Admittedly, it is a reformation that any lover of civilization must welcome : beginning near the Spanish Steps, the tide of cars has been steadily pushed back westwards towards the Tiber. But perhaps it has been carried too far : the shopkeepers of the Via Borgonna have actually gone to the expense of carpeting their street, creating in effect a hushed temple of money.

One young woman complained to me: "I get furious when someone walks up to me in the street, in my city, my Rome, and starts speaking a foreign language as though I were the alien." Her attitude, however, is by no means universal. Most Romans are quite inured to waves of babbling foreigners. They smile and shrug at best, stalk away or overcharge at worst, and go serenely about their own business knowing that in the end the "invaders" will be moulded by Rome—or leave, as others before them.

Rome's admittedly chauvinistic tolerance has been sorely tried in recent years by the annual migration of the world's transient youth—long-haired, caftaned, shawled, beaded, bearded and often unwashed. These wanderers drift down Europe with the summer sun, setting out from the north after Easter and ending up around Naples in late autumn. They migrate

In a shaft of sunlight American sculptor Robert Cook works in his studio, a former stable in a quiet courtyard below the slope of the Pincian Hill. Cook has lived and sculpted in Rome for 30 years, a successor to the many artists from other countries who have in every period flocked to join the city's artistic life.

instinctively to Rome en route. Huddled and clucking like pigeons on the Spanish Steps, they sprawl and sing, stack their gaudy paintings along the walls, lay out for sale, on tatty bits of velvet, their hand-tooled leather belts and their steel-and-glass jewellery. For most it will simply be a stopover, and no sooner have they arrived than they are gone, leaving behind nothing but strips of sticking plaster which they used to attach their velvet display sheets to the ancient stones. Romans, having stoically picked their way through these knots of untidy humanity now for several seasons, may mutter to themselves as they climb the Steps, but they are not unduly irate. For again, there has been no permanent effect on Rome or on their lives.

A few yards away, where the Via Margutta makes its way between high, dun coloured walls, lies an area that exerts a far more enduring pull on the foreigner. A century ago it was almost entirely given over to artists and sculptors to whom fashionable patrons would come, leaving their carriages at the corner and picking their way across gutters and heaps of rubbish.

The artists are mostly gone now, replaced by art galleries, dozens of them standing side by side. But a few painters and a few sculptors, still survive here. Halfway down the street is a row of battered buildings. If you go through their double doors, you step into a garden courtyard that is backed by the sudden green fall of the Pincio Hill. Worn steps wind through rich foliage growing between tiny cottages that cling to the slope. Roaring Rome is only a few hundred metres away, but the atmosphere is as peaceful as a remote mountain village. Along one side of the main courtyard, in full view of the hill, stand cavernous buildings. Once they were stables; now many are chic houses. From some you can hear the clink of metal on stone. These are the sculptors' studios.

One of the sculptors is an American, Robert Cook. He is part of a tradition that has kept Rome an art centre for centuries. And he is only one of many artists and writers who have come from abroad and made Rome their home in the last few decades. In an earlier age he might have travelled two to three hundred miles from Urbino, or Florence, or Perugia. But Cook arrived in Rome via Paris just after the Second World War, studying under the U.S. Veterans' benefit programme called the G.I. Bill of Rights. He found a studio in the courtyard off the Via Margutta and has stayed there ever since. He works just inside the big double doors, where the light falls exactly right. His medium is bronze, and he follows a process older than Rome itself. He moulds his statues first in wax, which he collects from the farms of the Campagna, melting it, colouring it, building it into sweet-scented forms. Then he has these cast in plaster and finally in bronze.

Robert Cook and his wife have a flat just off the near-by Corso, and a farm in the *Campagna*. They regard Italy in general and Rome in particular as home. They move easily in Italian circles: they can talk to their rural neighbours about crops and rainfall, or circulate with grace among the often-esoteric poseurs in the artistic salons of Rome. Yet they remain essentially Americans. On their weekends in the country they call on English and American friends in near-by houses, all of whom intersperse their English with more convenient Italian expressions. The Cooks sent the eldest of their two Roman-born children back to the United States to college. The girl in the end may remain in America, although she usually returns to Rome each summer holiday to see her family and savour again her adopted homeland.

In many ways this typifies the situation of most of Rome's legion of expatriates. (The English-speaking community alone is so large that it supports its own newspaper, the *Daily American*.) Over the past few years international organizations have multiplied in the city. F.A.O., the Food and Agriculture Organization of United Nations, employs more than 5,000 people in its gleaming white palace near the Circus Maximus. Their numbers are swollen by a horde of Diplomatic Corps families. Unlike other capitals, Rome has two sets of foreign diplomats: one to the state and the other to the Vatican.

Most of these international civil servants, and the scores of businessmen who represent multinational industrial complexes, lead a split life, often with a residence in their homeland and one or more refuges in Rome. In two years, four years, ten years, they become acclimatized—strangers in residence—who tend to look upon mere tourists with amusement or even contempt. They know that the gauche American will never find "a real down-home steak" nor the Englishman a proper "cuppa" until the Roman waiters and restaurateurs are ready to dispense such items. And that day seems a long way off. They know that no phalanx of blue-haired matrons will be able to purchase expensive clothing between 1 and 5 p.m. because the Roman shops still close during these hours. They know, rather smugly, that salt, stamps and tobacco are dispensed from the self-same shops because these are all state monopolies. They know that strikes, holidays, public protests, religious celebrations will go relentlessly on, with complete disregard for the wishes and sometimes the physical comfort of foreigners and residents alike. Most of all, they know that they are accepted in Rome to the precise degree that they accept. If they learn passable Italian, if they submit to the vagaries of custom, if above all they are successful in what they do but not overly aggressive in doing it, they will be welcomed, embraced, laughed with—instead of being laughed at. And yet they know that they will never be completely Roman.

The Fountains of Rome

The huge Trevi fountain is a magnet for visitors; in the belief that those who toss in a coin will certainly return, tourists fill it with 150,000 lire a day.

In Rome the sound of water is never far away. In grand *piazze* and obscure back streets it hisses, tinkles and thunderously cascades in noisy celebration of the extravagance and style with which the city has slaked its thirst during most of its history. Before barbarians destroyed the aqueducts that fed them, there were some 1,200 public fountains in Imperial Rome. After the Renaissance popes rebuilt the aqueducts, artists vied to create ever more elaborate settings for the presentation of earth's most basic liquid. Today Rome has more than 300 fountains of every size and shape, as the examples on these pages attest. They may no longer be needed for their centuries-old purpose of filling household jugs, but they are cherished by Romans as works of beauty, places to gather and—not least in importance —ready sources of clear, cool water on a hot summer's day.

To drink from a low-lying spout, a boy has to stoop.

A thirsty girl drinks from a 1,700-year-old fountain.

"Fidelity" reclines above one of four 16th-Century fountains that give the Via delle Quattro Fontane its name.

An inscribed shell and heraldic bees proclaim that this fountain, the work of Bernini, was a gift to Rome of Pope Urban VIII, a member of Barberini family.

Shining water pours from the muzzle of a bronze wolf.

At the Villa Borghese a rabbit's nose spouts water.

Outside the Pantheon, grotesque masks adorn a fountain erected in the 16th Century but redesigned in 1711.

A 15-foot-long bronze galleon fountain that fires a wet broadside is hidden in a Vatican garden, unseen by the public. It was made for Pope Paul V about 1620.

8

The Outer Reaches

Compared to Rome's present-day size of 582 square miles, the core of the ancient city is minute. Ninety per cent of Rome's three million inhabitants live in the outer areas. As in any large city, many of these later outgrowths are characterless, if not downright unpleasant. But some of them still maintain vivid rhythms of their own. There are two in particular that stand out sharply in my memory: one is the ancient, independent Trastevere, which huddles close to the centre but as its name states retains its separate identity as an area "across the Tiber". The other is the oddly-named E.U.R., which stands for *Esposizione Universale di Roma*. E.U.R. was planned by Mussolini in the 1930s as Rome's "universal exhibition" and as a new administrative centre for Rome, if not all of Italy. It came unexpectedly to life in the 1950s as a booming town in its own right.

The greatest and most obvious division in Rome is that imposed by the Tiber, which runs through the western part of the metropolis in a series of huge loops. As in many other cities that are divided by rivers (Paris' Left and Right Bank, Buda and Pest etc.), there are vast differences between the areas on each side of the river. Trastevere, across the river from the central city and hemmed in by the Janiculum Hill to the west, is distinctive in appearance, in atmosphere, in manners, even in dialect, from central Rome. Consider the church of S. Maria in Trastevere. It is splendid in medieval gold mosaics and inlaid marbles, but it is barely touched by the Roman passion for the Baroque. The square that fronts it is spacious, but it has the feeling of a small town piazza, with its tinkling fountain, its children on bicycles and the people who lean over the balustrades of their roof gardens high above the saffron-coloured buildings.

A blind person could tell when he had crossed the Tiber and left central Rome. Outside the centre there is much less traffic; what there is moves almost decorously. The vehicular traffic has even been known to give way to pedestrians. In Trastevere that is just as well, for the streets are narrow, most of them little more than alleyways (*vicoli*) winding steeply upon themselves, so that the most experienced urban explorer may lose all sense of direction. And during the lulls in traffic, the blind person would detect the difference in the speech around him, particularly in the speech of the gangs of adolescent males, whose talk consists mostly of amiable insults with a long-drawn, derisory "oooo" sound in the vowels.

Trastevere is full of hidden treasures. In the central city the great monuments have been over-exposed, so that sometimes one seems to be looking at, and often part of, an enormous cliché. But in Trastevere it is as well to

Like a huge, permanently moored ship, the Tiberine Island seems to ride Rome's river between the central city, on the left, and Trastevere, "Across the Tiber", on the right. The broken section of bridge in the background is all that is left of the first stone bridge over the river, built in the 2nd Century B.C.

be armed with a guidebook; for here it is as though the stream of history has piled up an obscuring silt. S. Maria in Trastevere is a 12th-Century Romanesque church, concealing a core so ancient that it is reputed to be the oldest church in Rome. Another church, S. Cecilia in Trastevere, a huge, much-renovated structure, is the supposed resting place of a famous 3rd-Century martyr, whose story is worth retelling. S. Cecilia, a high-born Roman, vowed to remain a virgin but was forced to marry a pagan. Apparently she was a woman of some force: she retained her virginity and converted her husband. She then set about distributing all her wealth to the poor, which so dismayed those in authority that she was ordered to be burned. The flames, however, had no effect on one so pure, and she was beheaded instead. Her gentle spirit seems remote from the bleak building that bears her name. But I like to think that it is preserved somehow by the church's quiet garden, with its pungent shrubs and murmuring fountains.

Near by is another unmarked historic site. In a side street an unremarkable door opens on to a private garden; you may trespass discreetly. When you do, you step into a garden of orange trees, flowers and tomatoes growing in a rich-smelling soil. The garden once belonged to Donna Olimpia, the famous virago described in Chapter Four who robbed her brother-in-law, Pope Innocent X, while he was on his deathbed. Legend has it that her spectre prowls the area, her huge pleated hood billowing in a ghostly breeze. Philanthropists acquired the garden and built an almshouse there which might account for the avaricious Olimpia's ghostly and irritated presence. Such historical footnotes have been well hidden by the dross of centuries. Perhaps the *Trasteverini* felt no need to recall them, the loss being made up by the strength of their own character and traditions. The people of the area, traditionally working-class families who eat as if in a village—at long tables, sharing their food and their rough local wine with friends and even, in high-spirited moments, with passing strangers—were always a proudly independent lot. They are, they claim, the "true Romans", whatever they think that means. In ancient Rome, Trastevere's gladiators were the toughest; in recent times their street brawls have been reputedly the most riotous, their songs the most lascivious, their women the most sensuous, and their alcoholic capacity the most amazing. Such, at any rate, is their boast, one that may be confirmed by a visit to an annual celebration of Trastevere's independence: The *Festa de Noi Antri*, the "Feast of Us Others". During the week-long *festa*, held at the end of July, the *Trasteverini* crowd into the streets to sing, eat and drink. Tables spill out of restaurants and block the traffic. Guitarists serenade diners. Waiters rush through the throng, bearing traditional dishes of roast suckling pig, watermelon and spun sugar. Hundreds of booths offer worthless trinkets. Petty criminals buzz around on Vespas, snatching purses. Riotous boxing and soccer matches are held. On the last day the proceedings are capped by a monumental fireworks display.

To avoid unnecessary stair climbing in the city's many old, high blocks of flats, Roman housewives—like this one leaning from a window—have devised their own technique for hauling groceries into their kitchens.

In some ways, of course, things are changing. The sturdy underpinning of small workshops tend now to be engaged in more artistic trades, for Trastevere has been "discovered". A few years ago, the majority of outsiders who lived here did so for simpler reasons: it was cheap. Then the area was found by those who were looking for "atmosphere" and were not so concerned with cost. The native population was driven out by inexorably increasing rents, and the fashionable, both Italian and non-Italian, moved in. But these despoilers are now chagrined to find the path they opened up being trodden by the middle-class masses.

In Trastevere's famous eating places, prices have soared and standards have fallen as transient diners opt for atmosphere. Outside one of the tourist restaurants I saw a sign in English: "Come and Get It! The best Chow in Town, Italian-style". The communal open-air meals still survive, but the paper tablecloth is giving way to linen, the flasks of yellow wine are being ousted by imported bottles, and the diners themselves are being edged into the outer darkness. The new setting looks attractive enough if you pass through in a hurry; but on closer acquaintance you find the gaiety hollow, with hired musicians and waiters who are victims of the conveyor-belt mentality. Trastevere shows only too clearly what could happen to Rome should it ever seek to please foreigners.

But these changes do not as yet go deep. Trastevere still has a peasant feel about it, for it is surprisingly close to the country. Ten minutes' walk brings you to the Janiculum Hill. The tree-clad lower slopes are largely a rubbish dump, but from the summit you can smell the farmyard manure of the fields along the Via Aurelia, and chickens cluck and cocks crow beneath the slopes where the Janiculum runs north towards the Vatican. All in all, it will be some time yet before the Trastevere is overwhelmed by central Rome, before the spirit of "us others" disappears.

E.U.R., three miles south of the Aurelian walls along the teeming, multi-laned Via Cristoforo Colombo, is a total contrast. It dates back only to 1938: Mussolini dreamed of turning the area—then 1,000 acres of pasture in the stillness of the *Campagna*—into an exhibition centre for a world fair, to be held in 1942. It would then, he planned, become the focal point for his new Rome, the "Third Rome" that was to overlay the imperial and papal cities. Gleaming white marble buildings, massive in the cardboard cut-out style of Italian Fascism, were already beginning to rise from the meadows when the Italian dictator's declaration of war against France and England in 1940 brought the work to an end. Four years later, the huge empty shells were severely damaged as the Allied troops swept up the Italian peninsula. The place remained a ghost town until the early 1950s, apparently ready only for the bulldozers.

Then, to house the burgeoning bureaucratic and residential populations of the city, Rome set about turning Mussolini's dream into reality. Government ministries, conference centres, company headquarters, museums,

Almost perfectly preserved in all its liveliness and grace, this stucco ceiling relief shows the abduction of a daughter of Leucippus by Castor or Pollux. It is one of a rich variety of scenes decorating the mysterious underground Basilica di Porta Maggiore, probably the temple of one of the mystic sects that proliferated in Rome between the 1st and 4th Centuries A.D.

residential areas, parks and spacious avenues turned E.U.R. into an independent entity, one remarkably similar in concept to the model devised by Mussolini. Today E.U.R. is a fashionable and very expensive township that is proud of its semi-autonomy and would like completely to break away from the Roman administration. Significantly, the initials S.P.Q.R. (*Senatus Populusque Romanus*) that appear on almost every piece of public property in Rome itself are replaced, on the belongings of this rebellious daughter, by the initials E.U.R. And these initials—pronounced roughly "aye-ur"—have already become accepted by the inhabitants as the area's fit and proper name.

Viewed from one of the near-by hills, the stone or glass towers that soar up from luxuriant foliage resemble all that the architect's model promised. Mussolini's contributions are unmistakable: enormous blocks tending towards but not quite achieving vulgarity. There is the huge church of Ss. Peter and Paul that sometimes looks like the Sacré Coeur in Paris and sometimes like the Taj Mahal; there are the disquieting, surrealist columns of the museums; and above all there is the weirdly impressive monster now known as the Palace of the Workers. This is the true symbol of Mussolini's

Newly-ordained priests from South-east Asia add special significance to their first mass by celebrating it in an old sanctuary, the Catacombs of S. Sebastian.

dream, a vast building whose ground floor arcades are stuffed with life-size statues representing virtuous abstracts.

E.U.R.'s thriving commercial life has contributed shops and cafés, so that the heroic has been tempered by the human. But even so, I do not find it a welcoming place. After Los Angeles, it must be one of the first localities designed on the assumption that man is no longer a walker but a driver. Distances are a little too great, the main roads too wide and shadeless to permit a casual stroll from one handsome amenity to another. Admittedly, all Rome has been conquered by the car, but E.U.R. has gone to the extreme of lunatic logic. Here, the cars on side roads are parked on pavements, coolly shaded by the trees while the pedestrians pick their way along the roads, braving the traffic and the sun's glare. I enjoyed strolling by the huge lake, listening to evening concerts in the open air and dining high up in a science-fiction structure that is actually a water tank. But I returned gratefully to the chaos of the mother city.

The Mother City. The concept is a grand and warming one, and parting from such a city is hard. I left it on a grey Monday in November. The scudding clouds had brought sharp showers and a sudden drop in the temperature; the wind howled through the streets; the warm olive of Italian complexions had turned sallow.

I had made myself a promise: that when I left Rome I would go on foot down the Via Appia Antica, the Appian Way, first of the so-called Consular Roads that linked Rome with its far-flung empire. It would be, I thought, a symbolic conclusion to my stay; for this narrow strip of ancient road, pounded by traffic and flanked by the detritus of modern suburbia, combines Rome's two worlds: that of the present and that of the distant past. I would send my luggage ahead and travel as the earliest travellers did, until I gained open country.

Now I was to keep that promise. The visible track of the Via Appia rose gently on the far side of the Piazza le Numa Pompilia, named after the Sabine king of Rome in the 7th Century B.C. Here the narrow road is asphalted, encased between ancient walls of grey stone. Behind the walls were pine and chestnut trees, azaleas and rhododendrons. I spotted the tombs of the aristocratic Scipio family, warrior-statesmen of the 3rd and 2nd Centuries B.C., and a little octagonal chapel that Romans call, matter-of-factly—*S. Giovanni in Oleo*—St. John in Oil. The chapel marks the spot where St. John the Evangelist is alleged to have emerged unharmed from a cauldron of boiling pagan oil.

This tunnel-like reach of the road debouches into the snarl of traffic through a narrow opening in the 3rd-Century Aurelian Wall. Now called the Porta San Sebastiano, the gate was once the Porta Appia, and from it the Via Appia descends gently between a jumble of ruined tombs, petrol stations and restaurants.

Every guide-book extols the Appian Way. Every guide-book insists that the only way of seeing it is on foot. But the writers of most such works must have compiled their notes in the back of a car. I had once previously tried walking the road to visit the celebrated catacombs that are strung along both sides of it, but I gave up in fear and rage. The Via Appia was built some two thousand years ago by the Censor Appius Claudius for traffic; it is still used for traffic, in spite of the fact that the flow has increased ten-fold in speed and a thousand-fold in density. The great, green buses of Rome, at least half as wide as the road, hurtle down it at top speed, pushing a mass of air before them as they go, sucking up dust and refuse in their wake. Private cars whizz past like bullets; careening trucks often scrape the walls as they roar along. So terrifying is this traffic that I temporarily abandoned my plan to walk, and instead boarded a bus.

Encased in steel and noise, I was whisked past sights I would have preferred to linger over. And it was with relief that I got out at the ancient catacombs of S. Callisto to resume my walk. I glanced back to behold a sight both sad and inspiring—the walls of imperial Rome, built not to protect a young and growing society, but an old and dying one. The Emperor Aurelian began to raise the 12-mile circuit in A.D. 271 against the incursion of barbarians, while the legions were fighting in distant countries. The work took nine years, and has survived for 17 centuries, in spite of the scars alike of Gothic siege-engines and of high explosives dropped from Allied aircraft during the Second World War. For at its core is the durable Roman concrete, and its face is composed of thin, red-brown bricks that have mellowed with time. From my vantage point I could also see St. John Lateran, the Cathedral of Rome, high on its plateau, the statues on its façade visible across the length of the city.

The Catacombs of S. Callisto stand in gardens filled with blood-red gladioli. These catacombs—places of burial for the earliest Christians—are one of the great tourist attractions, combining as they do a hint of the macabre with piety and historical interest. And here, even on parting from the city, I found Rome's capacity for paradox unabated. For considering the casual way in which Romans treat their churches—hucksters on the steps, loud-voiced guides in the interior and photographers clambering everywhere—I had expected a fairground approach to the Catacombs. But I found instead a deep, unobtrusive piety. The Catacombs now have electric lighting but the visiting groups are rigorously controlled—for the danger of being lost underground, of slowly going mad while trying to find a way out of this maze of the dead, is very real. The tens of thousands of bodies have long since been removed, but the narrow passageways and dark recesses still hold secrets. Occasionally the guide's torch picks out some poignant memorial—a hastily incised dove, a gentle farewell, a loving portrait badly done. The gaily-clad tourists, growing cold in that eternal chill, feel themselves intruders and return thankfully to the surface.

Laid two thousand years ago, the tightly fitted stones of the Appian Way, ancient Rome's most famous road, are still in service outside the city's southern wall. Beyond, where the grooves worn by ancient wheels begin to disappear modern tarmac takes over.

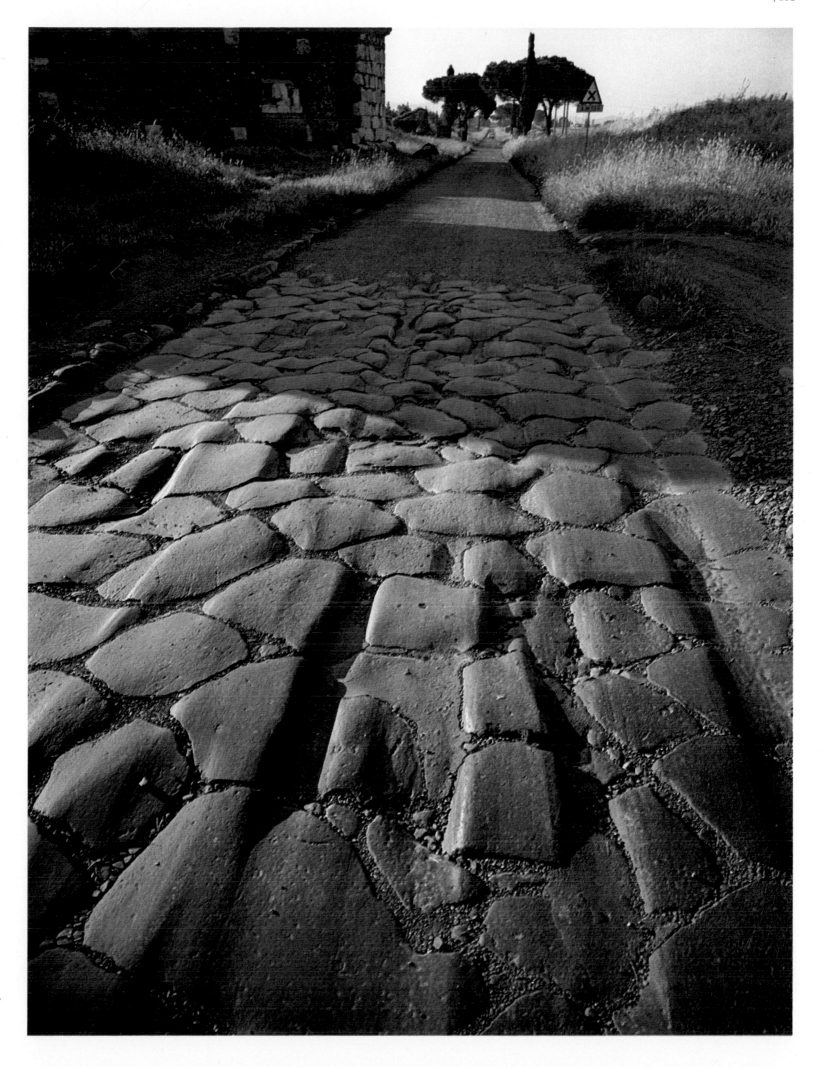

As for myself, emerging into the light and gazing again at the Rome that I had left, I felt as if I were standing between two eras. Before me, bristling with churches, was the foremost Christian city of the world. Behind me the Via Appia vanished across the *Campagna*. It was a fitting place for catacombs to be. For in these secret labyrinths the earliest Christians prayed and hid from persecution. Their dark warrens, filled with the bodies of saints and martyrs, saw the end of the old pagan capital and the emergence of the new Christian Rome. In this they are deeply moving, for they stand mid-way between the Imperial and the Papal—the city's twin greatnesses.

Now I turned my back on Rome and began to walk down the old pagan way. I passed the brown stone towers and sprawling mass of the Circus Maxentius, built in the 4th Century A.D. by the emperor Maxentius as a monument to his son Romulus. Before me the Via Appia rose up a slope, aiming arrow-straight at the tomb of Cecilia Metella, immortalized by Byron as "the stern round tower of other days".

I climbed the road and ventured across a plateau on which the ancient roadbed was marked not only by a thin ribbon of asphalt but also by the umbrella pines and tall cypresses that border it. Some trick of Roman traffic control interrupts the flow of cars along this stretch of the way: there are long periods of quiet, punctuated by sudden tidal waves of onrushing metal. As each swept towards me from the rear I stepped smartly to the side, on to the relative safety of the remains of Roman pavements, called *crepedines*, which still rise six inches higher than the roadbed. So must the ancient Romans have leapt for their lives at the approaching clatter of horses' hoofs and the iron-rimmed wheels of carts and chariots.

For a while the road ran straight, and every now and again the asphalt ended, so that I could see and tread upon the big grey basalt blocks that once paved it. They are enormous stones, laid according to order to last "forever". Plainly visible in their surface are the grooves made ages ago by rumbling iron-shod wheels. Walking along, I came to an abrupt bend in the road that afforded a view of two mounds on the right. These were small and undistinguished, but the Romans believed them to be the tombs of the Horatii and Curiatii, Roman and Alban soldiers of the 7th Century B.C. who fought and perished here. Modern scholarship tends to dismiss them as apochryphal, but in Appius Claudius's day, they were part of the tapestry of legend and faith, and the road bent around them from respect.

Once I had gone past the mounds, the track straightened again. This is the stretch visited only by lovers and tourists, neither of whom were much in evidence on this cold day. Here the Via Appia surprised me by being what it ought to be—haunted, remote, infinitely melancholy. True, on each side of it rises the new Rome, barely masked by shrubs and trees; and when I climbed the road's banks I could see on each side the raped land of the *Campagna*—an area of disused quarries, stagnant water, rusting machinery. It was a depressing sight, and I turned gratefully to the more evocative reality of the road itself. Across these stones marched the Roman legions. Here trudged St. Paul, on his way to Rome. Here Julius Caesar, as *curatore*, perhaps on a windy day like this, came out from the city to inspect the condition of the roadbed.

I was less than a quarter of an hour's journey by car from the city centre; yet I was a world away in spirit, two millennia away in time. By now it was the Roman "lunch hour", and I knew that I was relatively safe from traffic for the three hours of this daily hiatus. Then a single car appeared, halted not far from me, and two rough-looking men descended. I felt a twinge of fear, for all was empty, all was quiet. It turned out that the men had stopped for the most innocent and elemental of reasons, but that momentary fear demonstrated to me what the surroundings of this city must have been like a century ago, when brigands could strike with impunity. Or in Roman times, when feuds, rivalries and assassinations were culminated here with the certain knowledge that the news of them would travel swiftly back to Rome. It was not far from this spot that the Roman nobleman Milo murdered a relative of Appius Claudius, Publius Clodius Pulcher. It was a routine murder for its time, but one made immortal because Cicero defended Milo before the Roman Senate and later produced, in *Pro Milone*, one of the most eloquent works of the Latin tongue.

As I reflected upon all this, the car with the two rough-looking men moved off. The wind murmured in the pines. The day seemed suddenly colder, darker. Ahead of me the track of the Via Appia petered out into an unkempt, uninviting field. I turned to look back the way I had come. On either side of the road ruined tombs stretched like an avenue, back into the past—the past of Europe and of half the world. Rome had disappeared, hidden behind the thrusting new green growth of the trees that rise among the stones and the tombs.

The Vital Element

Gazing dreamily from an oval window, a round-faced child adds the asymmetrical touch of life to the perfectly-balanced façade of a peeling stucco palace.

Rome's history is so long and its layers of the past so rich that the city seems almost to have an existence of its own, distinct from that of the people who happen to live there. But every great city serves mainly as a backdrop for its citizens, and no view of buildings alone can ever be so arresting as one that includes the presence of people. The following pictures show how that presence, even if only a reference in the form of an effigy or a doll, can transform a cityscape from a lifeless vista to a vital drama. Even a fleeting glimpse of human figures—a child at a window, an aged man in a garden, a couple in quiet companionship, lovers embracing—brings with it implications of the constants of human experience: youth, age, religion, passion. In Rome, so old and so various a city, the scene of so many past lives, they have a special poignancy.

This flowery balcony, perched like a nest under the eaves of the Villa Doria-Pamphili, makes a dash of colour against the warm stucco. In its heart a couple dine in tranquil privacy.

A black-robed prelate, his eyes bent on the breviary in his hands, reflectively paces the hot, white paths of the Vatican garden, with its Mediterranean vegetation.

Pegged by its synthetic hair to the washing line next to a child's little dress, a gleaming modern doll displays its smooth plastic body against the crumbling wall of a block in old Rome.

Surrounded by presences charged with history, a custodian in the Vatican's Egyptian Museum turns his back on the cool, unpeopled gloom to gaze out into the blazing Roman day.

In a flamboyant little shrine, lacking many of the humble seashells from its decoration, a figurine of the Virgin Mary makes an archetypal gesture of compassionate resignation.

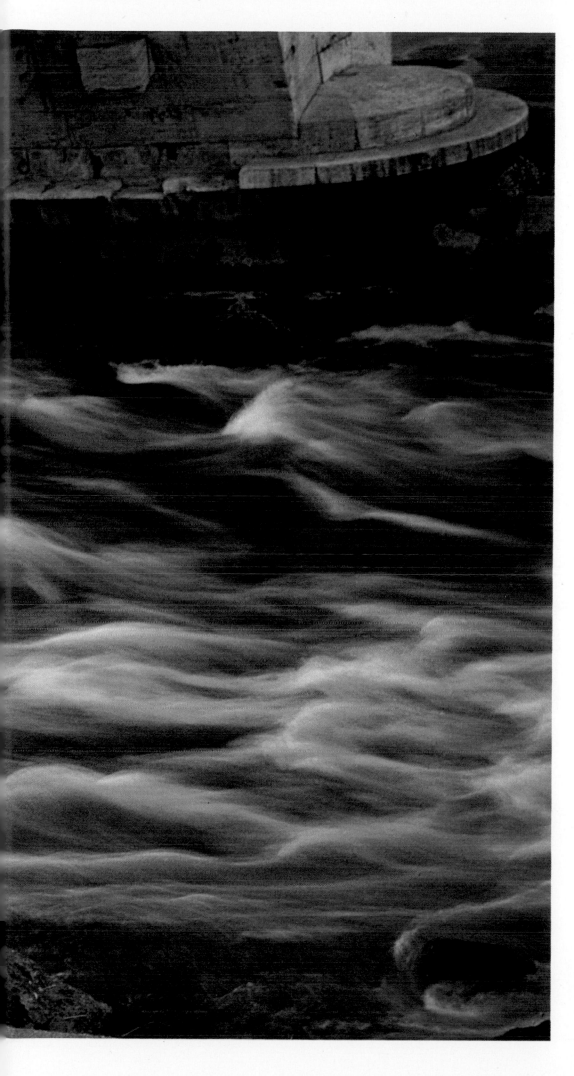

In the lee of a gigantic bridge pier, a pair of lovers, seemingly oblivious to the sound of the Tiber's rushing water, savour their total possession of one small patch of Rome.

Bibliography

Ackerman, James Sloss, *The Architecture of Michelangelo.* A. Zwemmer, London, 1961.
Balsdon, J. P. V. D., *Roman Civilisation.* Penguin Books, London, 1969.
Barker, Ethel Ross, *Rome of the Pilgrims and Martyrs.* Methuen & Co., London, 1913.
Bevan, Gladys Mary, *The Early Christians of Rome.* S.P.C.K., London, 1927.
Barzini, Luigi, *The Italians,* Hamish Hamilton, London, 1964.
Bittner, H., and Nash, E., *Rome—Portrait of the Eternal City,* Henry Regnery Co., Chicago, 1950.
Bolton, Glorney, *Roman Century 1870-1970.* Hamish Hamilton, London, 1970.
Bonechi, Edoardo, *Rome—A Complete Guide for Visiting the City.* Edizioni "Il Turismo", Firenze, 1973.
Brentano, Robert, *Rome before Avignon— a Social History of 13th Century Rome.* Longman, London, 1974.
Brizzi, Bruno, *Ancient Rome Yesterday and Today.* Casa Editrice Colombo, Rome, 1973.
Brizzi, Bruno, *Rome—Le Fontane.* Casa Editrice Colombo, Rome, 1972.
Brown, Peter, *Religion and Society in the Age of St. Augustine.* Faber & Faber Ltd., London, 1972.
Bryce, James, *The Holy Roman Empire.* Macmillan, London, 1887.
Burckhardt, Jacob, *Civilisation of the Renaissance in Italy.* Phaidon Press, London, 1951.
Carandente, Giovanni, *Rome—World Cultural Guides.* Thames and Hudson, London, 1971.
Crawford, Francis Marion, *Ave, Roma Immortalis.* Macmillan & Co., London, 1898.
Cronin, Vincent, *The Flowering of the Renaissance (3 vols.).* Collins, London, 1969.
De Tuddo, Italo, *Rome the Fourth Day.* Libreria Frattina Editrice in Roma, 1967.
Dickens, Charles, *Pictures from Italy and American Notes.* Chapman and Hall, London.
Gibbon, Edward, *History of the Decline and Fall of the Roman Empire (7 vols.).* Methuen, London, 1896-7.
Grant, Michael, *Roman Myths.* Weidenfeld & Nicolson, London, 1971.
Grant, Michael, *The Roman Forum.* Weidenfeld & Nicolson, London, 1970.
Gregorovius, Ferdinand, *History of the City of Rome in the Middle Ages (Vols. I-VIII).* G. Bell and Sons, London, 1900-9.
Hare, Augustus, *Walks in Rome.* Kegan Paul, Trench, Trubner & Co., London, 1913.
Hutton, Edward, *Rome.* Hollis & Carter, London, 1950.
Kirschbaum, Engelbert, *The Tombs of St. Peter and St. Paul.* Secker & Warburg, London, 1959.
Lanciani, R., *The Golden Days of the Renaissance in Rome, from the Pontificate of Julius II to that of Paul III.* Constable & Co., London, 1906.
Llewellyn, Peter, *Rome in the Dark Ages.* Faber & Faber Ltd., London, 1971.
Lubbock, Percy, *Roman Pictures.* Jonathan Cape, London, 1923.
Mann, Horace K., *Lives of the Popes in the Early Middle Ages.* Kegan Paul, Trench & Co., London, 1902-32.
Masson, Georgina, *The Companion Guide to Rome.* Fontana, London, 1972.
Marucchi, O., *The Evidence of the Catacombs for the Doctrines and Organisation of the Early Church.* Sheed & Ward, London, 1929.
Morton, H. V., *The Fountains of Rome.*
Michael Joseph, London, 1957.
Pastor, Ludwig, *The History of the Popes from the Close of the Middle Ages (40 vols.).* John Hodges, Kegan Paul and Co., 1891-1953.
Pius II (Aeneas Sylvius Piccolomini), *The Commentaries.* George Allen & Unwin, London, 1960.
Perowne, Stewart, *Rome from its Foundation to the Present.* Paul Elek Productions, London, 1971.
Quennell, Peter, *The Colosseum.* Newsweek Book Division, New York, 1971.
Rodocanachi, Emmanuel, *Le Château Saint-Ange,* Hachette, Paris, 1909.
Rossiter, Stuart, *The Blue Guide to Rome.* Ernest Benn, 1956.
Roth, Cecil, *The History of the Jews in Italy.* The Jewish Publication Society of America, Philadelphia, 1946.
Schultz, J., *"Pinturicchio and the Revival of Antiquity".* Journal of the Warburg Courtauld Institute (Vol. XXV), London, 1962.
Scherer, Margaret, *Marvels of Ancient Rome.* Phaidon Press, London, 1955.
Stobart, J. C., *The Grandeur that was Rome.* Sidgwick & Jackson, London, 1975.
Sumption, Jonathan, *Pilgrimage—An Image of Medieval Religion.* Faber & Faber Ltd., London, 1975.
Touring Club Italiano, *Roma e Dintorni.* T.C.I., Milan, 1962.
Trevelyan, George Macaulay, *Garibaldi's Defence of the Roman Republic.* Longmans & Co., London, 1907.
Wallace, Robert, *The World of Bernini.* Time-Life Books, New York, 1970.
Wittkower, R., *Gian Lorenzo Bernini—the Sculptor of the Roman Baroque.* Phaidon Press, London, 1955.

Acknowledgements

The author and editors wish to thank the following for their valuable assistance:
Ingegneri Bardi, Azienda Comunale Elettricità ed Acque, Rome; Anthony Blunt, London; Vatican Library, Vatican City; Countess Mita Corti, French Embassy, Rome; Giancarlo Danovi, Ministero Affari, Esteri, Rome; Charles Dettmer, Thames Ditton, Surrey; Superintendent Itala Dondero, Soprintendenza Alle Antichità di Roma, Rome; Douglas Fleming, The Daily American, Rome; Bianca Gabbrielli, Rome; A. Vinci Giacchi, Italian Embassy, London; Susan Goldblatt, London; Antionietta Grimaldi, Caffé Greco, Rome; Orazio Guerra, Ufficio Stampa del Comune, Rome; Dora J. Hamblin, Rome; Archbishop Bruno Heim, Apostolic Delegation, London; Jim Hicks, London; Sue Hughes, London; Father George Leonard, Catholic Information Office, Kings Langley, Bucks; Alta Macadam, Florence; Linnel McCurry, London; Marquis Ubert Pallavinci, Sovereign Military Order Knights of Malta, Rome; Monsignor Romeo Panciroli, Pontifical Commission for Social Communications, Vatican City; Commander Mario Pennacchi, Eliservizi Italia S.R.L., Rome; Walter Persegati, Director of Vatican Museums, Vatican City; Willy Pocino, Azienda Comunale Elettricità ed Acque, Rome; Signor G. Porro, Il Messaggero di Roma, London; H.E. Ambassador François Paux and Madame Paux, French Embassy, Rome; Karin Pearce, London; Anna Pugh, London; Lieutenant Hans Roggen, Swiss Guard, Vatican City; Signor Rossignoli, Farnham, Surrey; Deborah Sgardello, Rome; Paul Solomon, Rome; Colin Thubron, Uckfield, Sussex; Paolo Tournan, State Archives, Rome; Ludmila Tschakalova, London; Marjorie Weeks, Pontifical Commission for Social Communications, Vatican City; Alexandra Bonfante-Warren, Rome; Mary J. Wilson, Rome.

Index

Numerals in italics indicate a photograph or drawing of the subject mentioned.

Colour reproduction by Printing Developments International Ltd., Leeds, England—a Time Inc. subsidiary.
Filmsetting by C. E. Dawkins (Typesetters) Ltd., London, SE1 1UN.
Printed and bound in Italy by Arnoldo Mondadori, Verona.